NAVAL
ELECTRONIC
WARFARE

(Photograph courtesy of British Aerospace)

BRASSEY'S SEA POWER: Naval Vessels,
Weapons Systems and Technology
Series, Volume 5

Brassey's Sea Power:
Naval Vessels, Weapons Systems and Technology Series

General Editor: DR G. TILL, Royal Naval College, Greenwich and Department of War
Studies, King's College, London

This series, consisting of twelve volumes, aims to explore the impact of modern technology on the size, shape and role of contemporary navies. Using case studies from
around the world it explains the principles of naval operations and the functions of naval
vessels, aircraft and weapons systems. Each volume is written by an acknowledged
expert in a clear, easy-to-understand style and is well illustrated with photographs and
diagrams. The series will be invaluable for naval officers under training and also will be
of great interest to young professionals and naval enthusiasts.

Volume 1—Modern Sea Power
DR GEOFFREY TILL

Volume 2—Ships, Submarines and the Sea
DR P. J. GATES AND N. M. LYNN

Volume 3—Surface Warships: An Introduction to Design Principles
DR P. J. GATES

Volume 4—Amphibious Warfare
JAMES D. LADD

Volume 5—Naval Electronic Warfare
DR D. G. KIELY

Other series published by Brassey's

Brassey's Battlefield Weapons Systems and Technology Series, 12 Volume Set

General Editor: COLONEL R. G. LEE, OBE

Brassey's Air Power: Aircraft, Weapons Systems and Technology Series, 12 Volume
Set

General Editor: AIR VICE MARSHAL R. A. MASON, CBE, MA, RAF

For full details of titles in the three series, please contact your local Brassey's/Pergamon
Office.

NAVAL ELECTRONIC WARFARE

by

Dr D G KIELY

Foreword by
Admiral of the Fleet Sir Edward Ashmore GCB, DSC

**BRASSEY'S DEFENCE
PUBLISHERS**
(a member of the Maxwell / Pergamon Publishing Corporation plc)

LONDON · OXFORD · WASHINGTON · NEW YORK · BEIJING
FRANKFURT · SAO PAULO · SYDNEY · TOKYO · TORONTO

U.K. (Editorial)	Brassey's Defence Publishers Ltd., 24 Gray's Inn Road, London WC1X 8HR
(Orders)	Brassey's Defence Publishers Ltd., Headington Hill Hall, Oxford OX3 0BW, England
U.S.A. (Editorial)	Pergamon-Brassey's International Defense Publishers, Inc., 8000 Westpark Drive, Fourth Floor, McLean, Virginia 22102, U.S.A.
(Orders)	Pergamon Press, Inc., Maxwell House, Fairview Park, Elmsford, New York 10523, U.S.A.
PEOPLE'S REPUBLIC OF CHINA	Pergamon Press, Room 4037, Qianmen Hotel, Beijing, People's Republic of China
FEDERAL REPUBLIC OF GERMANY	Pergamon Press, GmbH, Hammerweg 6, D-6242 Kronberg, Federal Republic of Germany
BRAZIL	Pergamon Editora, Ltda, Rua Eça de Queiros, 346, CEP 04011, Paraiso, São Paulo, Brazil
AUSTRALIA	Pergamon-Brassey's Defence Publishers Pty Ltd., P.O. Box 544. Potts Point, N.S.W. 2011, Australia
JAPAN	Pergamon Press, 5th Floor, Matsuoka Central Building, 1-7-1 Nishishinjuku, Shinjuku-ku, Tokyo 160, Japan
CANADA	Pergamon Press Canada Ltd, Suite No 271, 253 College Street, Toronto, Ontario, Canada M5T 1R5

First edition 1988

Library of Congress Cataloging in Publication Data

Kiely, D. G. (David G.)
Naval electronic warfare.
(Brassey's sea power; v. 5)
1. Great Britain. Royal Navy—Electronic installations. 2. Electronics in military engineering. 3. Electronics in naval aviation. I. Title.
II. Series. VM480.5.G7K54   1987   623'.043   87-16057

British Library Cataloguing in Publication Data

Kiely, D. G.
Naval electronic warfare.—(Brassey's sea power. Naval vessels, weapons systems and technology series; v. 5).
1. Electronics in marine engineering—
Great Britain
I. Title
359.8   VM480.5.G7

ISBN 0-08-034757-6 (Hardcover)
ISBN 0-08-034758-4 (Flexicover)

Cover photograph courtesy of Plessey Marine

Printed in Great Britain by A. Wheaton & Co. Ltd., Exeter

Contents

Foreword

by

Admiral of the Fleet Sir Edward Ashmore GCB, DSC

This book on the application of Electronic Warfare in the Royal Navy is a welcome and timely review of its important subject. Communications Electronic Warfare has a respectable history since wireless came to sea in time for the Great War. Opportunities for intelligence on the one hand and concealment and deception, the prime ingredients of surprise, on the other were ingeniously exploited thereafter. I well remember the hard grind involved for the Fleet Wireless Assistant in the measures undertaken to conceal the movement of the Home Fleet in the 1940s. The impact of Radar on maritime operations soon became decisive leading, with Convoy, to the turn of the tide towards victory in the Atlantic in 1943. Preoccupation with the threat of the torpedo-armed submersible led the Service directly to the requirement for instant certain detection and bearing of Radar transmissions, however short, and the development of appropriate receivers is described with justifiable pride in this book. The very limited range of detection of these early equipments was itself tactically desirable, as was the low incidence of false alarms.

The United States Navy, influenced primarily by the requirements of the air war, had earlier developed lower probability high sensitivity equipments with which we were generously equipped, as with so much else, for the operations of our Carrier task force with the 5th and 3rd United States Pacific Fleets. Much was learnt. For example, air strikes were flown against Japan with chaff cut to suit the radars detected during the preceding attack. After the war, as development and production of equipment slowed and the wait for the UA1 became intolerable to some of us, various rather naughty expedients were initiated to keep the art of Electronic Warfare sufficiently regarded in the Fleet. Use of our own radars as directional receivers, conversion with the help of the Service Electronics Research Laboratory at Baldock of some naval air to surface radar for the same purpose, and the introduction of radar silence diagrams were among the measures adopted and exercised. The arrival of properly designed equipment thus found a surface Fleet not entirely lost to the subject and the submarine and air arms well aware of the potential and perils of non-communication electronic warfare. Security was still a bane; not until the middle fifties was British and United States expertise confided to the NATO Allies.

Moreover, the fitting of the equipment in a special wireless office, the unreliability of successive generations of ECM equipment and a reluctance on grounds of safety to attack ship-to-air communications all conspired to diminish the impact on the Royal

Navy's operational command at sea, giving the EW Controller less scope than he deserved. The coming of the missile changed all that and more beside. Exocet was fitted in the Royal Navy in the 1970s and by then some EW office equipment was being sited in Operations Rooms. While performance of the high probability direction finding equipments had advanced to meet the new threat, ECM lagged badly and remained unreliable. But the Command, in general, was alerted and reforms in the control of ship's operations rooms with the introduction of Warfare Officers and much delegation of authority proceeded apace. As Dr. Kiely indicates, the future lies with software and its ability to adjust, rewrite and adapt rapidly to changes in threat assessment. Providentially, the hardware which his book so well describes remains in step with the need. If I would stress one quality required of it more perhaps than he has done, it is the need for reliability. In the prosecution of Electronic Warfare confidence is all important, without it the necessary speed of reaction will not be attained.

In commending this book to the professional reader, it is right to draw attention to the outstanding qualifications of the author in his subject. David Kiely joined the Royal Naval Scientific Service in 1944, was Head of the Electronic Warfare Division at the Admiralty Surface Weapons Establishment from 1965 to 1968 following this by heading its Communication and Sensor Department from 1968 to 1972. Later he became Director General in the Ministry of Defence for successively, Telecommunications, Strategic Electronic Systems, Electronics Research and Naval Surface Weapons Projects, and finally The Chief Naval Weapons Systems Engineer. A fervent supporter, as I am, of the Application Officer principle whereby user, scientist and engineer all contribute to development, he has as broad a knowledge of his subject as man could and his down to earth commonsense approach, evidenced by his initiation of the Cardinal Points Specification procedure for defence equipment procurement, to which he refers in his book, make him an experienced, authoritative and percipient guide to this now vital field of maritime activity.

EDWARD ASHMORE

Acknowledgements

Acknowledgement is made of the use of material from the *Journal of Naval Science* Vol 7 No 2, Vol 8 Nos 1 and 2, Vol 4 No 2 and Vol 10 No 4.

Also acknowledged is material supplied by the Plessey Company, Marconi Company, Wallop Industries, Irvin Great Britain Ltd, British Aerospace, MEL, Thorn-EMI, Racal Electronics and Sperry.

The author is particularly grateful for information on HFDF from P G Redgment and wishes to acknowledge with gratitude the assistance of Elisabeth Goulding in the preparation of the manuscript.

In making this overview, there has been no intention that the comparative reviews of types of equipment should in any way be interpreted as a criticism or commendation of any particular system, component or material.

List of Figures

Glossary of Terms

AEW	Airborne Early Warning
AGC	Automatic Gain Control
AIO	Action Information Organization — the command centre in a warship
ALDIS Lamp	A form of naval signalling lamp
AMPLITUDE Comparison DF	A method of direction finding based on the amplitude of the signal received on two aerials
ARM	Anti-radar missile
ASE	Admiralty Signal Establishment
B DIENST	German Intelligence Organization in World War II
BITE	Built-in test equipment
CARDINAL POINT SPECIFICATION	A new form of specification used in defence procurement which states desirable operational and performance requirements.
CENTROID DECOY MODE	Use of a decoy to move the centre of a combined ship-decoy radar echo away from the ship.
CHAFF	Metallised filaments approximately half wavelength long released in a cloud to provide a radar decoy echo
CW	Continuous wave
DISTRACTION DECOY	One to attract a missile before it has locked on to a ship target
DUMP	A decoy to attract a missile when it has been pulled off a ship target
DYNAMIC Range	The extent of signal amplitude a receiver can accept between detection threshold and saturation
ECM	Electronic countermeasures
ECCM	Electronic counter-countermeasures
ELINT	Electronic Intelligence
EMCON	Emission Control
ERP	Effective Radiated Power
ESM	Electronic Support Measures
EW	Electronic Warfare
FH3, FH4	HF Direction Finding sets used in World War II
FIFO	First-in, First-out buffer: an electronic circuit
FPB	Fast Patrol Boat
GHz	Giga Hertz — frequency units of 10^9 cycles

HF	High Frequency — in the range 1 to 30 MHz
HFDF	High Frequency Direction Finding
IFM	Instantaneous Frequency Measurement
INTERCEPT Probability	The probability that the intercept equipment will detect a transmission (usually short in duration) which is above its sensitivity threshold
ISRM	Inverted Scan Rate Modulation
MCMV	Mine countermeasures vessel
MMI	Man-machine interface
MHz	Mega Hertz — frequency units of 10^6 cycles
PRF	Pulse repetition frequency
PRI	Pulse repetition interval
RAM	Radar Absorbent Material
RAM	Random Access Memory
RCS	Radar Cross Section — a measure of the size of the target in producing a radar echo
RF	Radio frequency
RGPO	Range Gate Pull-Off
RMS	Root mean square — a statistical measure of accuracy
SEDUCTION DECOY	One which draws a missile off a ship target to which it has locked or is about to lock onto
SFM	Spin Frequency Modulation
SRM	Scan Rate Modulation
SSRM	Swept Scan Rate Modulation
STEALTH	Steps taken to avoid radar detection by equipment design or operational employment
TOA	Time of Arrival
UA1 to 10	A range of radar intercept equipments covering different frequency bands.
UHF	Ultra High Frequency — in the range 200–400 MHz
VHF	Very High Frequency — in the range 30–200 MHz
VLF	Very Low Frequency — in the range 3–30 kHz
WT	Wireless Telegraphy

1

Introduction

Within the field of naval weapons and sensors, there is a clear and generally appreciated role for most of the principal elements. Guns, missiles and torpedoes are for attack and inflicting damage; radar and sonar are for detection; navigational aids help to determine position. The role of electronic warfare (EW) is perhaps less well understood although the term is familiar and its importance in naval operations has now grown to major proportions. What electronic warfare actually is, and how it is conducted, has been shrouded in secrecy in the past. It is really only in quite recent times that some aspects of the subject have become a matter for public discussion and debate.

In essence, electronic warfare is the practice of technical opportunism and expediency, exploiting weakness in an enemy's use of electronics for his weapons and sensors, and cleverly taking advantage of features of enemy equipment design or his use of electronic equipment. Electronic warfare has come about entirely through the ever increasing use of electronics in naval operations and it has proved to be potentially very powerful in gaining tactical advantages.

It is, however, unlike other naval weapons and sensors in that it is basically a reactive rather than a direct activity. It reacts to what the enemy does in the design and use of equipment, to the intelligence knowledge available on his equipment and to the way it is used. Thus the nature of electronic warfare is quite different from the use of other weapons and sensors, and it might therefore be thought to be essentially secondary and trivial in its effect. This is certainly not the case. Electronic warfare has now evolved into an element of naval operations which is important, commands the expenditure of considerable funds, and has now a structure and established practice of its own, as will be discussed in the chapters which follow. Despite the obvious need for secrecy, enough can be said about the general principles and typical equipments used to give an understanding of the methods and importance of electronic warfare in modern naval operations where the Royal Navy has played a pioneering role.

Today all navies use electronic warfare to some extent. In the major navies it is well established and plays a leading part in their conduct of operations at sea. Even in smaller and less sophisticated navies engaged in relatively simple operations there is advantage to be gained from the use and principles of electronic warfare. The defence equipment industries of the world provide a wide range of EW equipment ranging from simple and inexpensive devices to extremely sophisticated and expensive equipments, and all of this finds a ready market. Research and development activity in both Government and industry laboratories is extensive, and is essentially self-generating.

A new EW capability leads to compensating changes in design in weapons and sensors, which in turn lead to different EW equipments as a reaction. Leapfrog progress in this manner continues with an increasing spiral of complexity and cost, and navies have available to them a continuing source of EW equipment with a wide range of performance and capability to use in their ships, submarines and aircraft.

Essentially electronic warfare consists of three elements:

Making use of enemy transmissions for own ship's benefit, known as Electronic Support Measures—ESM or Passive EW

Spoiling enemy transmissions for his ship's use, known as Electronic Countermeasures—ECM or Active EW

Preventing the enemy spoiling own ship's transmissions, known as Electronic Counter-countermeasures—ECCM

and the subject can conveniently be discussed under these three headings.

In the early post-war days, whilst High Frequency Direction Finding (HFDF) was appreciated, anti-radar electronic warfare in the United Kingdom was regarded as something of a secret oddity in the context of defence equipment and operational doctrines. Although EW had a few enthusiasts, viewed by others as rather eccentric, it was not taken very seriously, though it was agreed that on occasions it could possibly be tactically useful. It was not seen as an important element in defence equipment for sea, land or air battles as it was felt it could not be relied upon since it depended upon intelligence information and enemy reaction to its use. However, this was really an expression of the lack of understanding, at that time, of the growing dominance of electronics in the conduct of warfare and the control of weapons.

Among the Services in the United Kingdom, the Royal Navy was the first to appreciate that electronic warfare had a very definite potential in a number of important areas. It could give very early, and in many cases the earliest, warning of an enemy presence through intercepting enemy radar and communication transmissions, and utilizing such phenomena as electromagnetic scatter and duct propagation. By analyzing the characteristics of radar and other intercepts, it offered the only means other than by visual observation, of obtaining information on enemy identity.

It was capable of detecting enemy radar before the radar detected the ship or submarine. And it could be a very cost-effective and (on occasions) politically acceptable method of reducing the lethality of enemy weapons by jamming or deception. Much to the credit of the naval officers concerned, and to the benefit of EW, the Royal Navy took electronic warfare seriously from the start and began to study and plan its incorporation into the fabric of naval tactics as a weapon and sensor sub-system in its own right. These early beginnings led to the major position that EW now holds in the weapon complement of a ship, and to the striking success it achieved in the Falklands War.

Electronic warfare equipment was developed to achieve operational objectives. Because the frequency of radar signals to be intercepted was always uncertain, a wide band of frequencies had to be monitored. In Britain, the design philosophy was to do this by using broad-band receivers which gave continous coverage of the span of frequencies; this necessitated the design of broad-band aerials and other components. In the United States, however, the design philosophy was to cover the required frequency span by narrow-band scanning receivers which, because of their narrow-band width, had a higher sensitivity—but they gave an intercept probability of much less than 100 per cent.

For direction finding, the design philosophies of the United Kingdom and the United States were also different. The Royal Navy's equipment used fixed aerials and amplitude comparison direction finding techniques. The United States Navy, on the other hand, used narrow beam width rotating aerials which again gave a probability of intercept of less than 100 per cent. For frequency measurement, an important British invention, known as Instantaneous Frequency Measurement (IFM) was based upon broad-band phase comparison techniques while the USN equipment gave frequency measurement from the known tuning position of the scanning receiver when the enemy signal was intercepted. Both the broad-band and the scanning techniques are effective and both pose particular difficulties and problems but the RN's broad-band equipment has been most successful and its design has evolved into a very potent naval capability. Today the RN passive electronic warfare systems are very sophisticated but they employ the same basic broad-band techniques which were created for EW use in the 1950s.

Active electronic warfare has also developed both in technology and in operational use. The earliest concepts of noise jamming were soon found to be dangerous when applied against surveillance radars and missiles as it identified the user as a warship to surveillance radars and also provided a homing beacon for radar-guided missiles. Noise jammers gave way to more sophisticated decoys and deceptive measures. However, the evolution of ECM provided a positive spur to ECCM (the counter-counter-measures used by radar to give immunity to ECM) and the development of each technique has influenced the other as they grew in sophistication. Nowadays the specific ECCM features of radars are extremely important and also most secret as knowledge of them would reveal the vulnerabilities of the radar to ECM.

Electronic warfare against communication signals has also been developed to a high degree of sophistication and is used to gain information from messages, to detect the presence of an enemy and to measure his strength. This has stimulated the development of encryption to conceal message contents and also the development of other methods of transmission, such as short bursts and weak signal techniques, which are difficult to intercept and locate.

In the underwater field similar techniques are used and these may be called Sonic Warfare since electromagnetic waves are replaced by sound waves in water as the form of transmission. Passive sonar is a sensor of major importance to submarines. It is used to intercept active sonar, the noise generated by the propulsion of an enemy vessel and by the passage of its hull through water. Noise reduction in surface ships and submarines is of great importance as this constitutes a form of involuntary transmission which can be detected at quite long ranges by enemy sonic warfare equipment. In electronic warfare there is no comparable involuntary transmission and ships and submarines can make themselves silent to enemy EW by switching off their electromagnetic transmitters used for radar or communications. Active sonic warfare is also carried out through the use of decoys which may take the form of bursts of air bubbles released under water, or other more sophisticated forms of false signal generation. As noise reduction improves then active sonar transmissions become more necessary since there is little or no involuntary noise to intercept, and this active sonar then makes the user vulnerable through revealing his presence and direction. Thus the balance of tactical advantage and disadvantage must always be assessed. The submarine attempting to avoid active sonar detection must be made to have as low an echo as possible and this has led to coating the hull with material which tends to absorb rather than reflect sound waves from a sonar; there is a parallel in electronic warfare where similar non-reflecting material is used against electromagnetic waves from radar.

In modern ships electronic warfare is now a firmly established and extremely important area of naval weapons and sensors. From early beginnings of a mixture of enthusiasm, doubt, distrust and tactical vision EW has shown that it can contribute most significantly to naval operations. Although some degree of enemy involuntary co-operation is necessary for success —the enemy must use electromagnetic transmissions, but then he has to to fight his ship—the balance of advantage is strongly in favour of EW yielding a tactical contribution. There are now naval officer EW specialists and an EW Branch within the navy to provide a continuity of experience and expertise which is in itself an expression of the important role played by this essentially opportunistic type of naval weapon and sensor system. It is of course, primarily necessary to involve the Command in ships in the practice of electronic warfare and it is intended to encourage and facilitate this by the provision of specialist operators and sub-specialist officers to give a depth of knowledge available to the Command.

Naval electronic warfare has an important contribution from naval aviation and the maritime aircraft of the RAF. While the EW impact of the Fleet Air Arm and the RAF is fully recognized and acknowledged, the part they play in naval electronic warfare is not treated separately or in any depth in this book for reasons only of limited space. Nevertheless, EW involving aircraft in maritime operations is very well developed and practised both in support of and against ships in operations at sea and in training. It is integrated into the overall concept of naval electronic warfare and it is important both in ESM and in ECM for offence and defence.

The first enthusiasts gave the navy an early and valuable start in a new type of warfare and the maxim which they coined—one can't win a war with EW, but one can't win a war without it—is perhaps even more true in the present day than it was thirty years ago. Such is the consequence of the major and growing dependence upon electronics in all the other branches of naval weapons, sensors and communications.

2

The Early Days of Naval Electronic Warfare

While interception and DF of naval communications was practised and was important in World War I as an early form of radio warfare, naval electronic warfare as it is known today in England really began in the Second World War. Prior to this, there were some isolated incidents involving the interception of messages which could be seen as incidental or accidental forerunners to electronic warfare, and these included events leading to the Battle of Jutland. But the deliberate and planned practice of naval EW did not really start until the wartime years, and even then it was not known as electronic warfare in the sense that the term embraces today. Nevertheless, this early EW scored an important success in the form of HF direction finding against German U-Boat transmission in the Battle of the Atlantic.

An excellent account of the early stages of evolution of naval electronics, including radio warfare, is given by Admiral Hezlet in his book *The Electron and Sea Power* (Peter Davies Ltd, 1975), which includes some examples of initial steps in what is now known as electronic warfare. These constitute an effective introduction to the beginning of the more general and deliberate practice of EW in the Royal Navy in the 1940 decade, starting with the widespread use of shipborne HF DF which will be our starting point here.

HF DF AGAINST SUBMARINES

In the early days, DF was used not for electronic warfare but to assist navigation and the plotting of bearings was considered part of the navigation process, rather than as an extension of DF. During the Second World War, however, the development of large specialised DF networks caused a change of emphasis, the operations of taking bearings and plotting them being treated together as a scientific experiment designed to locate a source of electromagnetic radiation. This outlook was adopted by most DF services but the arrangements devised were strongly influenced by individual operational needs, and differed between such services.

HF DF gave a warning of, and a direction for, the presence of a U-Boat which was using its HF communications to report the detection of a convoy and to summon other submarines to form a Wolf Pack. The use of HF DF by convoy escorts was singularly successful in initiating anti-submarine searches. In a way, it acted as a long range warning device before sonar was employed for shorter range detection in the final phase of the engagement.

The HF DF equipment operated mainly on the HF ground wave and employed Bellini–Tosi crossed loops with a sense aerial which had been developed by Admiralty

5

scientists. Research and development was carried out at the Admiralty Signal Establishment (ASE) at Lythe Hill House, Haslemere from 1940. Much excellent work in this field was done by a number of Polish engineers and scientists who had managed to leave Poland and offered their services to the Royal Navy. They were meticulous and dedicated in their development work and contributed significant advances to the field of naval HF DF particularly in relation to the reduction of site errors caused by parts of the ships structure.

Such was the importance of HF DF that the aerial shared with the radar aerial the prime site at the masthead. Indeed, any other site would have been disastrous for the crossed-loop aerial as the ship structure contained many elements of a length which resonated at the HF frequences in the 1–30 MHz band, and which would therefore have caused major errors with a DF aerial mounted lower and amongst them.

Equipment development, and applied research were extremely rapid in those days. New equipment and modifications could be brought into service at sea in months, rather than years. Most of the laboratory work, development, and drawings for production were carried out in-house at Haslemere and extensive workshops could manufacture small quantities of equipment for ships very rapidly. HF DF was, operationally, a great success and it represents the first real beginning of EW employed by a large number of ships. It is interesting that this start of EW was in the field of communications when subsequently virtually all the effort and application of EW was directed to radar signals. But at this time in the early 1940s naval radar had hardly begun, and it was appropriate to regard HF DF as a primary sensor against the U-Boats. It shared this role with radar when the first radar sets were fitted, and tended to be overshadowed by the success of radar at sea.

The fundamental problem that faced enemy submarines was that of the detection and location of convoys. This was as it had been during the First World War. One source of high quality intelligence on convoy movements was the interception and decryption of signal traffic relating to convoy organisation. RN cyphers had been broken in pre-war days by the German B.Dienst intelligence organisation and thereafter they had the facility to gain considerable amounts of information on convoy and escort movements and rendezvous intentions. This could then be utilised by the submarine controlling authority ashore to coordinate attack operations. This advantage continued until 1943 when the British introduced an unbreakable cipher and the B.Dienst had to start afresh.

The principal source of convoy vulnerability lay in radio transmissions as radio communication facilities in ships were far more prevalent than during the previous war. Initially, strict radio silence was the policy, the ships using flags and sirens by day and Aldis lamps by night. Radio silence could, of course, be broken when an attack was thought to be imminent or had actually broken out. Problems arose, however, when aircraft began to assist in escort duties and it then became essential to use High Frequency (HF) radio communications on a more regular basis. Although the equipment was of low power and was credited with only a horizon range it proved to be a valuable source of intelligence on a convoy's position as it could be monitored by enemy shore direction finding (DF) stations. This source of information provided approximate positions of the convoy which would then be passed by the submarine operating authority to whichever submarines were operating in the general area.

The next step for the submarine was to locate the convoy. Aircraft were one option providing their bases were not too far distant from likely convoy routes and the aircraft themselves had an adequate endurance. For example this technique was used in July 1940 when enemy bases were established at Brest and BV 138 flying boats with a range of 1000 miles were able to patrol the Atlantic to the South of Ireland. A month later FW 200 bombers became based at Bordeaux and with their range of about 2000 miles were even more suited for locating convoys for the submarines. The main advantage in using aircraft for locating convoys was the high rate at which they could search large areas of ocean compared with the submarine.

The submarines were not equipped with radar and their only means of locating a convoy was by visual detection, possibly backed up by information from HF DF ashore and hydrophones. By the end of the war, the development of the latter had progressed to the stage where a submarine at 100 feet was capable of detecting a convoy or large warships up to fifty miles away, depending on the environmental conditions at the time. The information was however limited to bearing information. The all important requirement for ranging the ships could not be met as active sonar was not fitted. Purely visual means of location were rather limited especially for an individual submarine. An escort or merchant ship as part of a convoy could be expected to be sighted from a submarine at a range of about 10 miles in daylight though funnel smoke from the ships could increase this range providing the atmospheric conditions were suitable. Only during darkness was the submarine denied this aid and then the location problem was made worse by the fact that the visual distance for an unlit ship falls to about a mile. From this point of view, the situation was little changed from the First World War.

Thus unless a single submarine was initially well placed with respect to the future track of a convoy it was poorly equipped to locate it by visual means. The problem was eased by the introduction of the 'patrol line'. This involved a number of submarines being deployed to form a line of bearing across the likely line of a convoy. The line would move at slow speed, about four knots, with the submarines keeping a visual lookout. The length of patrol line would vary with the number of submarines that were available and the conditions prevailing at the time. For example, in January 1943 a line of 450 miles in length was established by fifteen submarines in order to intercept convoy HX 223. In March 1943 an even longer one of 500 miles was set up using twenty-eight submarines against convoy HX 229/SC 122.

Arranging patrol lines did however generate radio traffic between the submarines and their operating authority ashore and this in turn made them vulnerable to interception by Allied DF stations. The fact that such a line was being assembled could therefore be discovered, or at least inferred, from radio intercepts. Such information could be passed on to the Escort Group to forewarn them of impending action. Alternatively it could lead to a diversion in the convoy route to try and outflank the submarines.

Experience in the 1914–18 war had indicated that a single conventional submarine was relatively ineffective against a properly escorted convoy. In building up his new U-boat force in the late 1930s Admiral (then Commodore) K. Doenitz sought to overcome this by devising tactics for group attacks by several submarines (or 'Wolf-Pack' tactics, as they were known). The system seems to have been fairly well advanced by the outbreak of war, but the circumstances for its effective employment did not arise immediately. Once introduced, these tactics were refined continuously as the war progressed.

The essential problem in co-ordinated operations by submarines arises from the need for communications. These are difficult to and from submerged boats and may compromise the covert nature of their operations. The arrangement adopted depended on long-range HF radio from boats on the surface, using signals propagated by reflection from the ionosphere. Except for some instances where MF signals were used for homing, there was normally no direct communication between boats. The transmission from a U-boat was received ashore and then re-broadcast, together with any other essential information, to the other boats of the group.

This system, although apparently clumsy, had several advantages. The shore 'control' transmitter could broadcast on several frequencies, receipt of such transmissions by the U-boat would indicate a satisfactory path was 'open' on the given frequency. This received signal could be used as a frequency reference, the transmitter being tuned either exactly to it, or offset by a (small) pre-determined amount. One end of each link could have large directional aerials and equipment that was not constrained by consideration of space and power. More than one shore station could listen for the necessarily low power U-boat signal. These stations could listen continuously so that the U-boat could transmit at any convenient moment; conversely the message could be re-broadcast several times, at agreed listening periods, and on several frequencies—including, if required, VLF for submerged reception.

The ship-borne direction finders then available did not cover the HF band and, whilst the risk of shore DF was recognised by the Germans, they apparently considered that this could be kept within acceptable limits by good signal discipline and by keeping the transmissions brief through suitable coding. The signal content was considered to be adequately protected by the use of the ENIGMA cipher machine. To ensure brevity, standard message formats were used, and it was possible to recognise the type of signal by its prefix. The most important example of this was the 'sighting report' made by a U-boat when a convoy was detected; the pre-fix was a Greek 'beta' sent twice, which in English morse equates to $\overline{B}$ (B bar). Hearing this prefix, the convoy was warned of an impending attack.

Since all communication passed through the shore organisation, it was both practical and convenient to execute tactical control of the U-boat group from shore. Probably the most important signal was the first 'B bar' contact report, but U-boats were also required to obtain permission before attacking, to avoid interference between boats of a group (probably particularly necessary if pattern-running torpedoes were used) and to report results afterwards. Such signals were all brief—perhaps 10–15 seconds—but other, longer, signals, reporting such matters as fuel and ammunition states, were also made although these could be made at times chosen to minimise the effect of DF. U-boats also used the system for weather reporting, which was vital to German forecasting.

The HF transmissions were thus an essential element in Wolf-Pack tactics and it was rapidly appreciated by the RN that they provided a possible point of vulnerability. Shore HF/DF could give approximate positions, and thus help to keep the submarine plot up to date, but more significantly, if escorts could be given a suitable HF/DF they could obtain advanced warning of possible attack, and be able to take appropriate action.

Although those directly concerned with the work had no doubt of the value of HF/DF in the 'Battle of the Atlantic', it was overshadowed by other devices, particularly Radar, in immediate post-war assessments. There seems to have been a number of contributing reasons. The general fitting of ship-borne HF/DF was roughly contemporary with the introduction of centimetric (S-band) radar, which was so successful in many fields that it was natural to assume that it dominated the U-boat war also. The Germans were unaware of the use made of HF/DF and tended to speculate that all unexplained attacks resulted from some form of Radar. Thus, when German documents became available after the war, they seemed to confirm the pre-eminence of Radar detection. Detailed analysis of convoy actions indicate that HF/DF played an important part in the defeat of the U-boat. More recently the release of British documents under the '20 year rule' has made it possible for a German Naval Historian to make a more complete analysis. In summarising his conclusions on ship-borne HF/DF, Rohwer states that: *'If we analyse the great convoy battles between June 1942 and May 1943—including both those operations the Germans regarded as successful and those that ended as either a minor success or failure—the remarkable fact is that the outcome depended decisively on the efficient use of HF/DF.'*

Two types of receiving equipment were developed and employed operationally. The first, the FH3, was of the aural null type and was in due course superseded by the FH4 using a twin-channel (Watson–Watt) receiver. The aerial systems were identical except that FH4 required an auxiliary loop at forty-five degrees to inject a lining-up signal. For early experimental installations, aerials without loops, originally intended for FH3, were modified in the model shop, but later this was included in production aerials used with either system.

FH3 was developed in parallel with the aerial system, making the maximum possible use of existing equipment and technology. It is a good example of the approach described by Sir Robert Watson-Watt as 'the cult of the third best'—the aim being to have an effective HF/DF operational at sea in the shortest possible time.

A good HF goniometer was available from the earlier work and this was incorporated. The receiver was based on a high quality communication receiver produced by Marconi's Wireless Telegraph Co, which was given the Admiralty reference B21, the input circuits being modified to match the gonio and switching provided to introduce the sense signal when required. This was arranged to change the connections to the field coils so that the minimum signal of the cardioid produced by the addition of the sense signal corresponded with one DF null and the maximum to the other. A second position interchanged the maximum and minimum. Thus by leaving the gonio on the bearing and comparing the signal strength in these two positions it could quickly be determined whether the bearing set was correct or reciprocal.

Installation of these sets, in production form, started in the latter part of 1941, the fitting rate building up rapidly in 1942; although at first minor production difficulties with the aerial caused some delays, the planned output had been attained by the summer of that year. The sets continued to be fitted until superseded by FH4 in 1943.

Following on from the original work of Watson-Watt, the Plessey Co had, by 1940, developed a commercial version of the Twin Channel DF with a cathode ray tube display, the Plessey RL66A and this formed the basis for the development of the naval receiver used in FH4. The work was carried out jointly by a group at ASE—and the Plessey Co's research laboratories, working very closely together.

The first experimental installation was made in 1941 not long after the first fitting of FH3. This was in HMS Culver, formerly a US Coast Guard Ship of the 'Lakes' class (others of this class were fitted with FH3). A painstaking programme of detailed development was, however, required before an acceptable performance could be obtained reliably.

By the Autumn of 1942, numerous escort vessels in Western Approaches Command had been fitted with FH3, the first production equipment and destroyers, sloops and rescue ships were all due to be fitted at first opportunity. Much valuable experience had been gained and some success in the battle with U-boats had been achieved by means of even this somewhat primitive equipment.

Without the provision of U-boat W/T frequencies and schedules from intelligence sources, no such progress could have been made. Moreover, considerable skill and discretion had to be applied when using this set and luckily some most able and experienced operators were applied to this task.

On intercepting a U-boat transmission and getting a rough bearing, the Captain could be asked to bring the ship round to bows-on or stern-on to the bearing as the accuracy would by markedly improved thereby. Before doing this, the operator had to decide, if possible, whether the signal was 'ground wave' or 'sky wave', not always easy with this set. The former indicated a local and possibly dangerous threat, whereas the latter was not necessarily of immediate interest.

A HF/DF bearing of a nearby U-boat was the first step in a successful attack, the next being radar, followed by sonar and finally depth charge, 'Hedgehog' and possibly the gun.

As far as German HF/DF was concerned, there was apparently no equipment on German ships and all their work was done by shore stations. Fixed U-Adcock systems were developed that used more than four aerials, since this permitted the size, and thus sensitivity, to be increased whilst still keeping the instrumental ('octantal') error small. Although such systems had been proposed in Britain there was no development here or in the United States until the German use in operational stations was discovered. Simple buried U-feeder systems were used and one would expect the polarization errors to be larger than the British DF's on all but exceptionally good sites.

Aural-null receiving systems were generally employed. A modification of the twin-channel CRDF, which made provision for automatic balancing of the channels, avoiding the need for the multiplicity of pre-sets used in the British receiver, was at a fairly advanced stage of development at the end of the war. It does not, however, seem to have had any operational use.

The concept of space averaging, which the British 'group system' sought to exploit, was approached in a rather different way in Germany. Instead of several normal DF aerials they experimented by increasing the size (in optical terms the 'aperture') of a single aerial system, thus averaging a larger section of the wavefront. There were several proposals under investigation but perhaps the most advanced was the 'Wullenweber' circular array. This promised a significant improvement in shore HF/DF accuracy, but the 'teething troubles' had not been overcome at the end of the war.

For ships having no VHF radio-telephone equipment, internal convoy communications were carried out at a frequency around 2.5 Mhz, and the Germans claimed that the propagation of the surface-wave over seawater was sufficiently good for transmission made in the area south of Iceland to be received on a Beverage aerial at a particularly favourable coastal site. They installed two such aerials at a suitable spacing and, by measuring the phase difference between them provided a DF with a high instrumental discrimination over a limited arc. It is not clear whether this gave results of any operational value, it seems likely to have been more of a scientific toy, but it is an indication of the danger inherent in any radio transmission.

While the subject of HF DF embraced much activity in equipment research and development, and gained a most considerable amount of operational success during the Second World War, it was not regarded as a part of 'electronic warfare'. It was not seen as one facet of a general, and much wider subject which included all the ways, active and passive, of exploiting the enemy's use of electronics.

The term 'electronic warfare' had not yet appeared and the total concept of EW as a new naval discipline had not been appreciated. HF DF against submarines was an isolated activity and, remarkably, the Germans did not realize that shipborne HF DF was being used against them; they thought it was impractical and only employed shore based DF themselves. Yet it was truly a most successful application of EW as it is known today, and it was the first major operational success of naval EW. Not until after the war did the first use of a new term appear widely in naval circles; this was 'radio warfare', a precursor of electronic warfare and its words clearly reflect the origin of EW in radio and communication activities rather than in radar, with which it is so much concerned today.

Strangely too, the modern form of twin-channel, cathode ray tube DF system was rooted in the academic research into radio atmospherics of Robert Watson-Watt whose academic work also produced the concept of radar. He has left a remarkable legacy in being responsible for the basic foundation of these two electronic devices which made such a major contribution to the winning of the war. Since then radar has continued to evolve into a sensor of vast importance for civil and military applications, but HF DF has decreased in significance largely because HF communications are now being used in ways which do not present such opportunities to EW.

Although used for special purposes today, HF DF does not enjoy the great operational significance it commanded during the war. But it made a great contribution when the opportunity was there to do so, and it served the Royal Navy well as the first true application of electronic warfare. Today HF intercept and DF must not be undervalued. The interception of the sighting report of a reconnaissance aircraft or a submarine alerting its base may be the first indication of an enemy attack to come, and the HF band is much used by Eastern Bloc countries.

ANTI-RADAR EW

When naval radar, and also airborne radar, became more established in the second half of the 1940 decade, attention started to be given to radar interception. The first equipments consisted of little more than waveguide horn aerials with simple crystal-video receivers. The horns were held in the hand and pointed in various directions around the azimuth. When a signal was intercepted, it produced an audible note in headphones. The audible note was at the radar pulse repetition frequency and the bearing of the signal was the direction in which the horn was pointing. The receiver sensitivity was about -40 dbm and this was enough to give an intercept range somewhat greater than the radar range on all but the largest radar targets. Submarines used these simple equipments to give warning of airborne radar when they were on the surface. Since the enemy radar frequencies could never be known accurately, it was necessary to make the intercept receivers capable of covering a band of frequency. In Britain the type of design selected to achieve this was a wide band, non-scanned, crystal-video receiver; in the United States the basic design was a frequency scanning superhetrodyne receiver which covered the band by scanning a narrow frequency gate across it. This basic difference persisted for many decades as the receivers became more complex. Today, the designs of modern radar intercept equipment still use broad band, non-scanning techniques. To increase receiver sensitivity microwave amplifiers were placed before the crystal detectors, and travelling wave tubes were the first to be used before solid state amplifiers were developed.

Direction finding was achieved by circular arrays of (initially four) fixed aerials operated in an amplitude-comparison method of determining the bearing of the signal. In the United States the method preferred was to rotate a pencil beam around the azimuth, which constituted another significant difference in EW equipment design. The British equipment, wide open in frequency coverage and in azimuth coverage had an intercept probability of one hundred per cent which the American equipment, although more sensitive, did not have, except at shorter intercept ranges. Much research in microwave propagation was carried out in Britain to see how the performance of tropospheric scatter and atmospheric ducts could be used to gain long range interception and a considerable body of new information on propagation was obtained.

Great attention was given to achieving wide frequency band performance in aerials, amplifiers and microwave components and very striking successes were achieved. Probably the most significant British contribution to EW techniques was the invention, in the Mullard Research Laboratories, of the Instantaneous Frequency Measurement (IFM) device. This was a broad-band microwave circuit which, by a phase comparison method, was able to measure the frequency of a radar signal on a pulse-by-pulse basis. It still dominates the design of radar intercept equipment today.

At the end of the war, captured German equipment appeared and it was surprising how very similar intercept equipment designs had evolved independently in Britain and Germany. Of particular interest was the German use of dielectric rod aerials for radar interception as these, very new, techniques were also at that time being explored in Haslemere for use by the Royal Navy. They gave a very wide frequency coverage as the electromagnetic transmission mode they used (HO1) had no frequency cut-off, unlike other waveguide modes.

Tunable search receivers for communications and radar information gathering and signal analysis were also developed, as were equipments for measuring radar signal characteristics of pulse width, pulse repetition frequency and aerial rotation rate which with the radar microwave frequency, constituted a 'fingerprint' for the radar.

In these early EW days, some attention was given to noise jammers for naval application, mainly to deny range information to gunnery radars, but other forms of ECM, such as decoys and electronic false targets, had not yet appeared on the scene. The jammer development was later based on a new type of valve known as a carcinotron which gave a wide bandwidth and enough output power to screen large ship targets. With much enthusiasm, intense laboratory activity and a lot of sea trials and tests in naval exercises, it became clear that the various aspects of what is now known as electronic warfare had a significant potential contribution to naval tactics, and that the emergent microwave and electronic technology was capable of providing worthwhile equipment.

At that time, up to about 1950, EW activities were separated in different parts of ASE. The Royal Navy then made the very wise decision to take EW seriously and all EW activity, both equipment development and naval application, was drawn together as a separate subject in the early part of the 1950 decade. This really was the beginning of naval EW as it is known today. It came of age at that time and thereafter its evolution, in both technical and tactical directions was fast and successful. It was based on a sound foundation of exploratory tests and trials, and it was always carried out in a close dialogue and friendly rivalry with the United States Navy in particular, and also with European navies. An informal electronic warfare 'club' came into being, and the EW community was always closely knit and well co-ordinated by various Official Groups which met and exchanged information. Today, there is still a very strong and flourishing EW Society known as the Old Crows, and the subject of EW continues to grow in naval importance, in the financial resources devoted to it, and in technical complexity.

During these early years the laying of the foundation of naval EW was much assisted by a close working partnership between the scientists and naval officers in determining where, within naval operations at sea, EW could play a part, and the optimum type of equipment to use in ships. This resulted in a very direct path to effectiveness of EW in ships, and in turn this led to an early measure of confidence in EW and a willingness to use it. At that time EW was very new; with poor and unsuitable equipment, naval acceptance of EW could have been delayed for years, and it is a tribute to the relationship between naval officers and scientists that EW was quickly and successfully integrated into the fabric of naval tactics.

The earliest electronic warfare equipment to be widely fitted in surface ships as a standard item was a simple, but effective, intercept and DF outfit known as UA1. It operated in the 10 centimetre band and had later additions covering the 3 and 6 centimetre bands. It consisted of four horn aerials per band mounted in a circular array around the mast, the receivers were of the crystal-video type without RF amplification and the display was a cathode ray tube on which intercepted radar signals appeared as radial lines indicating the directions of the radars. The method of direction finding was amplitude comparison and a loudspeaker gave the audible note of the radar pulse repetition frequency. There were no signal analysis facilities but operators became quite skilled at timing the radar aerial rotation rate and aurally assessing the pulse repetition frequency.

It was fitted in a large range of ships and used mainly for early warning of ships and aircraft. For many naval officers, it was their first experience of electronic warfare at sea. It soon became clear that the first, and earliest, warnings came from UA1.

A similar equipment, known as UA4, was fitted in submarines and here EW played a vital role as the only means of giving warning of airborne radar when the diesel-electric submarines of the day were charging their batteries and had some parts of their structure exposed to radar detection above water. The submarines came to rely upon UA4 very critically for air warning and it is true to say that this was the first really important role played by EW in the Royal Navy.

The simple UA1 was followed by much larger and more sensitive equipments which used broad band superhetrodyne receivers and were known as UA8, 9 and 10. The method of DF was the same four-channel amplitude comparison system used in UA1 but the increased sensitivity gave more range and there were facilities for isolating signals and analyzing them. Comparing their characteristics with those in a library of known radar 'fingerprints' gave the identity of the radar and from this the type of ship or aircraft carrying it could usually be deduced. This was an important step forward, since it provided the only means for the ship, short of a visual sighting, of obtaining target identity. However, sensitive broad band receivers in a ship using radars in the same frequency band suffered serious interference and it was necessary to use what was known as pulse blanking. This is a technique whereby the EW receivers were switched off for the duration of each radar pulse just before the radar modulator fired, and as a result the EW screens were cleared of the interference. Of course strong radar signals from nearby ships could not be blanked in this way, and EW receivers had to be designed with very large dynamic ranges to reduce the chance of them being overloaded from this type of interference.

The first anti-ship missiles, such as the STYX, were not sea-skimmers like EXOCET and they homed to their targets using steerage in both the horizontal and vertical planes. Sea-skimmers do not steer in the vertical plane; they use an altimeter to maintain a fixed vertical height in their trajectory. Against the earlier missiles, like STYX, an interesting type of decoy was used. Known as the masthead repeater this received the signal from the missile radar, amplified it and sent it back to the missile from a high gain masthead aerial which was pointed downwards to illuminate the sea surface some distance off the ship. The missile then saw both the ship and the reflected signal from the sea surface forming a composite target; it steered to the centroid of this composite target and would hit the sea short of the ship. This decoy was never used in action, and it is not effective against sea skimmers, but it is interesting as a device with some potentially valuable qualities; it has an indefinite duration of effectiveness, it is not expendable and so does not 'run out of ammunition' and it is carried on board the ship.

Early forms of chaff decoys dispersed from rockets were used in the 1950s and were quite effective as radars at that time could not differentiate their echoes from those of real ships. Noise jammers were also fitted, but as the threat of naval gunfire became outdated, so did these jammers as they had only one main function in denying range information. Their role in obstructing surveillance radars was always accompanied with the potential danger they introduced to the jamming ship by providing a homing beacon for missiles.

In the years after 1960, the Royal Navy acquired an increasingly sophisticated fit of electronic warfare equipment. The solid state age was getting underway, automatic data processing was becoming available at lower costs and with much greater capacity, and EW equipment made full use of this technology, especially for signal analysis and comparison with stored libraries of radar characteristics. Electronic warfare was by now fully accepted as a naval capability and was gaining more successes in exercises. The full impact of information technology was yet to be felt, providing, at relatively low cost, the very considerable degree of data handling capability and artificial intelligence which is such an important feature of today's EW equipment.

What was, in effect being forged in these early days was a new type of naval capability which was quite different in nature from the traditional, and well understood weapons, sensors and communications equipments which ships used to fight at sea. Electronic warfare never gave a definite promise of success. It did not have a guaranteed performance because it always depended upon the enemy doing something—he was required to transmit to be detected and he was required to have equipment which could be jammed or decoyed. Electronic warfare was therefore an investment in a potential which might, and usually did, pay off. It was, however, a safe bet, since the influence of electronics on naval weapons and sensors was growing at a phenomenal rate and more and more of ships' fighting capabilities were dependent upon electronic control. And the electronic control mechanisms have always had weaknesses and areas of vulnerability to exploit through suitable forms of electronic warfare. While it is little more than thirty years since it began to be generally and seriously used in ships, there is really no doubt that electronic warfare is here to stay as a new and different naval capability which can pay very significant tactical dividends.

EW has given rise to a new form of intelligence information gathering, known as ELINT to collect the raw material used in such operations.

All major countries engage in this activity to acquire the electronic signatures of potential enemy equipments and to compile the libraries of recognition information used in tactical EW. Special equipment is required for these collection activities and this strategic information is a necessary support for tactical EW. Nowadays the amount of electronic information of this type to be processed is enormous and the full capabilities of modern information technology are used, and indeed are required.

Electronic warfare now involves the entire electromagnetic spectrum used for weapons, sensors and communications; it extends to the infra-red bands and many of the EW techniques have been used with sound waves under water. The vehicles employed for naval EW are not only ships and submarines but aircraft and satellites. All navies, to some extent, engage in electronic warfare and the fact that it is a flourishing naval activity is testimony to the real tactical advantages it continues to provide.

THE ROLE OF INDUSTRY

In those early days of electronic warfare, industry played little part in the research and development of equipment. In the beginning, in the late 1940s, all the conceptual work, the laboratory research and virtually all the development was carried out in the Admiralty Signal Establishment at Haslemere. Indeed, most of it took place in huts built on the cricket pitch and in the cricket pavilion at Lythe Hill. This was in keeping with the general practice to do all research and development in-house, the need in this instance being reinforced by the fact that EW was then very secret indeed and little, if anything, was known about it outside the Service. Industry did make some components, such as microwave valves, but the equipment design was produced entirely in-house. All the development, up to the final sets of production drawings, was usually handled by the Establishment. Only when the numbers of equipments required were too great for the Establishment workshops to cope with was production handed over to industry. EW at that time was very much a closed and exclusive affair.

After the war, a slow change took place and more work was placed in industrial laboratories, notably the Mullard Research Laboratory and the GEC Laboratories, which began to make very useful contributions. But the overall equipment design concepts were still originated inside the Establishment and the prime contribution of industry was to design components and assemble the specified equipments into working entities. All production was carried out in industry, and gradually all the development too with only the initial conceptual work carried out in-house. Industry was quite widely and fully involved in naval EW by the end of the 1950s and was making a substantial contribution to it guided by the Establishment's scientists and the Application Officers. All the industrial work was done on the basis of detailed technical specifications and cost-plus contracts. Later, as the complexity of EW increased, Government scientists were reduced in number, and exports of naval EW equipment grew in importance, a very major change took place which placed even the conceptual stages of the work and the early research in the hands of industry. This became feasible because the technical capability of industry in electronic warfare had evolved to such an advanced degree that the Royal Navy could depend entirely upon its supply industry to provide a satisfactory capability in the concept and design of naval EW.

Now, in the 1980s, EW equipment is produced for the Royal Navy by a radically different process. Cardinal Points specifications, which are statements of the main performance features desired in EW (or other) equipments or systems, are prepared in a very general and non-mandatory manner by the Ministry of Defence. These are issued as a basis for fixed-price competitions and firms tender for production equipment to meet as many of the Cardinal Points as possible. All the concept, design and development work is done in industry and separate contracts for research and development are very few and restricted to particularly secret or non-exportable equipment. This new regime in the procurement of naval electronic warfare equipment has brought many advantages with the RN obtaining new equipment much more quickly, and in many cases at lower prices, because the technology is chosen by industry to be economical and cost-effective. Industry's role in naval electronic warfare has changed very considerably; indeed naval EW has now become quite big business in the world market and warrants the investment of considerable industrial resources for research and development. In Britain it is all, however, based on the sound foundation laid by the Royal Navy and the Admiralty Signal Establishment some thirty years ago.

3

Passive Electronic
Warfare – ESM

As a contribution to naval command and control, the interception of enemy transmissions can give two elements of important tactical information, warning and identity. While it is thus opportunistic, in that it depends upon a degree of enemy 'co-operation' the probability of achievement is high as radio and radar silence imposes a serious tactical limitation on the enemy. With suitable intercept equipment having adequate sensitivity to receive microwave signals by the scatter and atmospheric duct modes of propagation, a ship can obtain very long range warning, up to several hundred miles, by intercepting enemy radar transmissions. No other shipboard electromagnetic sensor can provide such long ranges. Submarines with some part of their structure exposed rely strongly upon EW intercept equipment for a warning of searching radars. The interception range of airborne radar is greater than the radar range on the submarine and it can submerge before detection.

The RN equipments, broad band and non-scanning, provide an intercept probability of 100 per cent against even short radar transmissions and in this respect have proved to be tactically very effective against radars attempting to avoid detection. Against impending attacks by radar homing missiles, such as Exocet, the intercept equipment can indeed give the only warning as sea skimming missiles are below the cover of ship's radar. Warning of enemy airborne surveillance is also frequently only given by EW interception. Thus the tactical benefits from radar intercept equipment can be enormous. Similarly, the interception of communication signals can also confer significant tactical advantage, particularly if the transmissions are not encrypted and provide information from their message content.

An interesting refinement of intercept techniques is provided in submarine equipment where assessment of the danger of detection posed by an intercepted airborne radar is very important. The range of the radar from the submarine cannot be reliably estimated because of the wide variations possible in the propagation path due to ducting or atmospheric absorption. But the point in time when it could detect the submarine can be estimated since this does not involve the propagation factor. This is, tactically, what is actually required and the process of determining this point in time is known as Reciprocal Intercept.

EW interception will continue to succeed as a naval sensor mainly because ships and aircraft of all types are now so dependent upon electromagnetic waves for surveillance by radar, for weapon direction and guidance and for communication and data exchange in command and control. To impose electromagnetic silence for long periods would constitute a major tactical limitation. Thus the balance of advantage in this aspect of electronic warfare lies with EW interception, provided that the intercept equipment is designed to be proof against simple anti-intercept measures, such as short transmissions. The basic design philosophy of RN equipment provides for this and has proved its value in exercises and operations over the years.

DIRECTION FINDING

From a tactical point of view, the interception of an enemy transmission is very much more valuable if the direction of the signal is also obtained. All the radar intercept equipment is provided with a DF capability and some of the lower frequency communication intercept equipment is also capable of direction finding. The great contribution made by HF DF in the Battle of the Atlantic against German U-Boats discussed earlier was probably the first significant tactical use of DF in naval warfare.

Nowadays more significance is attached to DF against radar signals. RN equipment uses multi-channel amplitude comparison techniques with fixed aerials giving 360 degrees coverage which can be incorporated into or around the topmast structure of a ship and into a submarine mast. With very wide band frequency coverage and a response to virtually all polarizations of the intercepted signal, the DF accuracy cannot, fundamentally, be high and the bearing information is not used for weapon direction. But it is used as a valuable indicator in general, all-round surveillance and for correlation with other sensor information. It gives the direction of a threat to within a few degrees and allows attention to be focused in the appropriate area. The DF contribution to command and control is thus not one of precision but one of general clarification of the threat appreciation and of discrimination between different intercepts of the same type of signal. More DF accuracy would be useful in correlating EW contacts with others from radar but this poses a difficult technical problem in relation to the very wide frequency band coverage of the EW equipment. This might be solved by using a second stage of high accuracy, tunable, narrow band, DF equipment.

Amplitude-comparison direction finding is so basic in the approach to electronic warfare that a clear understanding of its principles of operation is important. Referring to Figure 3.1, there are four identical aerials with broad radiation patterns mounted to point in the directions north, south, east and west. Together they provide complete 360 degree coverage in the azimuth with the radiation patterns of adjacent aerials overlapping each other such that the null of one coincides with the maximum of another. Each aerial is connected to an identical receiver and the outputs of the receivers are connected to the four deflection plates of a cathode ray tube. A signal arriving from the direction P is received by the N and W aerials and, depending on the direction of P, the signal strength in the N and W aerials varies. The ratio of the N and W signals, or their amplitude comparison, is a measure of the direction P.

This is shown on the cathode ray tube as a radial line Q of which the orientation is approximately equal to the direction P when the shape of the radiation pattern is appropriate. With practical microwave aerials, radiation patterns can be obtained which yield bearing errors less than 10 degrees and sometimes less than 5 degrees. This is the simplest arrangement to give complete azimuthal coverage with a minimum number of aerials and receivers, or 'channels', and it is known as a four-channel amplitude comparison DF system. There is no scanning; the four aerials continuously cover all directions and the receivers are wide-band in frequency coverage. So the system will 'see' any signal above its sensitivity threshold which arrives from any direction and is within the frequency band. It is said to give 100 per cent probability of intercept.

Bearing accuracy can be increased by using eight or sixteen aerials in a circular array with a corresponding number of receivers and appropriate circuit arrangements to display the signal as a radical line on the cathode ray tube. In more sophisticated equipment, while amplitude-comparison DF is used with eight or sixteen channels a

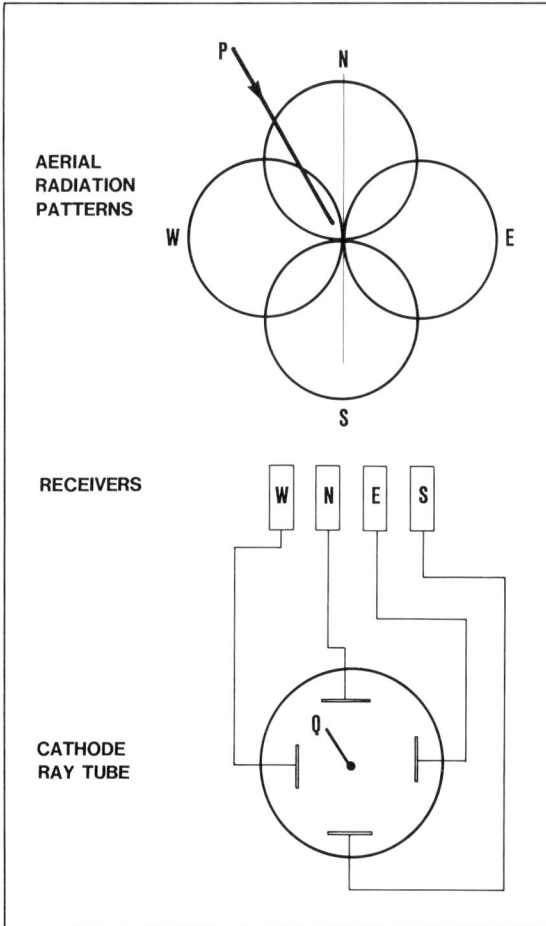

FIG. 3.1   Amplitude Comparison Direction Finding

different form of display can be employed to show both the bearing and the radar frequency. This is a rectangular form of presentation on a cathode ray tube in which the bearing is shown along the horizontal axes and the frequency along the vertical axis. An intercepted radar is shown as a spot on a set of Cartesian or rectangular co-ordinates where the x co-ordinate of the spot indicates its bearing and the y co-ordinate indicates its radio frequency. Bearing accuracy of some 2 degrees or better can be obtained from eight or sixteen channel systems operating over frequency bands of at least one octave and using aerials which will accept both vertical and horizontal polarization. This is representative of the very good performance currently available from this type of equipment supplied by British companies.

SIGNAL ANALYSIS

Probably the most important tactical information obtained from the interception of enemy signals is that relating to target identity which comes from analysing the signal characteristics. The radio frequency, pulse width, pulse repetition rate and the aerial rotation rate of a radar signal constitute a form of signature to identify the radar when compared with intelligence information on enemy radar characteristics. With the radar identified, the ship or aircraft carrying it can be determined and so the threat posed may be assessed. No other means, apart from visual observation, of identifying a target are available to the command in a ship and so this contribution of EW is of vital importance in many tactical situations.

Techniques for the rapid and accurate measurement of radar signal characteristics have been developed to a considerable degree of sophistication, together with software-aided methods of comparing these characteristics with a library of known radar parameters. The result of this analysis, either in the form of a positive or probable identification, is then associated with the bearing. It is available to the command as a valuable addition to the threat picture and perhaps for correlation with contacts obtained by other means. The EW analysis equipment can also be programmed to recognize and give immediate warning of nominated, specific threat radars which pose potential dangers that require a very quick reaction, such as Exocet.

Analysis of the structure and content of communication signals can also yield valuable information for command and control. While the methods used for this are rather more varied, the basic contribution of this form of electronic warfare remains unique and potentially very important for the command.

The processing and analysis of radar signals to gain target identity is a complex and important aspect of electronic warfare. It is discussed below in rather more detail to give some understanding of the nature of the problem and the great strides which have been made in equipment design to achieve successful analyses. These processing capabilities are at the heart of all modern, sophisticated ESM equipments.

PRINCIPLES OF ESM SIGNAL PROCESSING

Signal analysis as a means of assessing target identity is such an important feature of all modern ESM equipments that a general discussion of the principles involved, as seen in the Racal EW Laboratories, may help to provide a clear understanding of this important function of electronic warfare.

The key functions of a radar ESM system are outlined in Figure 3.2. The ESM system first receives radar pulses emitted by the various radars in the scenario, measures the parameters of these pulses, and then uses those parameters to sort out from which of the radars the pulses emanated.

Finally, the emitter is identified and information is presented to the operator. In order to understand the operation of an ESM system, it is necessary first to consider how a radar works. An ESM system is effectively a passive radar receiver, which picks up the pulses transmitted by the various radars in the environment and uses the parameters of these pulses to determine which radars are present. The receiver is designed to cover a wide parameter range to ensure detection of all radars of interest. From identification of the radars present, an inference is then made as to which platforms are present in the scenario and of their deployment.

Figure 3.3 shows a schematic diagram of an ESM system in operation. At the top left of this figure can be seen a traditional surveillance radar, which emits pulses of radar frequency energy, and then measures the time delay between transmission of the pulse

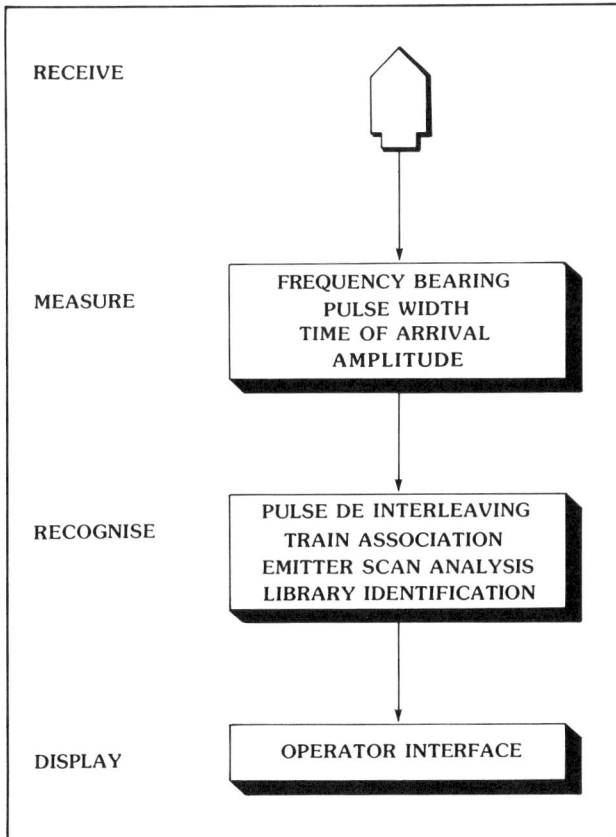

RECEIVE

MEASURE

FREQUENCY BEARING
PULSE WIDTH
TIME OF ARRIVAL
AMPLITUDE

RECOGNISE

PULSE DE INTERLEAVING
TRAIN ASSOCIATION
EMITTER SCAN ANALYSIS
LIBRARY IDENTIFICATION

DISPLAY

OPERATOR INTERFACE

FIG. 3.2   Key Functions of a Radar ESM System *(Racal Radar Defence Systems)*

and reception of echoes of the pulse from targets in the area to determine the range of those targets. To function correctly, the transmitting antenna must have a narrow azimuth beamwidth, and hence the direction of the antenna gives the radar the angular position of the target. In focusing the beam to produce as narrow an angle of transmission as possible, the antenna forms not only a mainlobe pattern but also sidelobe patterns, which are also shown in this figure. In operation the radar antenna rotates to give the required azimuthal cover.

Now consider the ESM system placed within range of the radar, as depicted in the bottom right of Figure 3.3, to determine what such a system will receive. First of all, consider the amplitude distribution received by the system. Imagine the antenna rotating past a diagonal line (shown on the figure) to determine what amplitude pattern

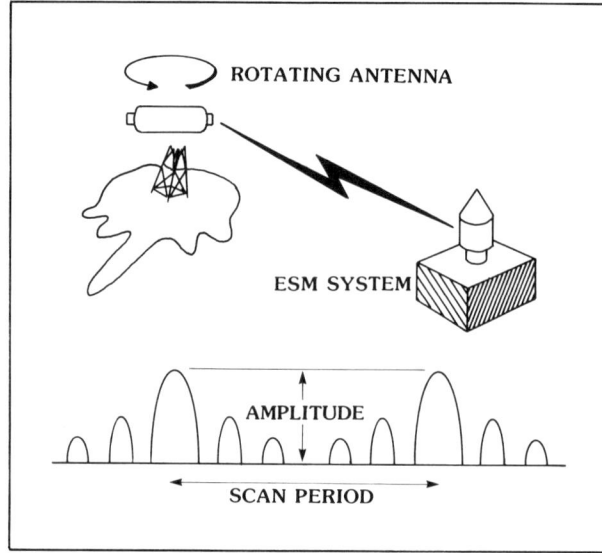

FIG. 3.3   Operation of an ESM System *(Racal Radar Defence Systems)*

is received. In practice, the ESM system will see the antenna radiation pattern unfolded in time, say, starting with the sidelobes, followed by the mainlobe and then the other sidelobes. This amplitude distribution for a single scan cycle is then repeated at the scan period of the radar. The amplitude envelope received is a series of pulses modulated by the radar frequency carrier. As a consequence, an ESM system positioned within the reception range of the radar will receive a number of short pulses of Radio Frequency (RF), whose amplitude distribution follows the antenna pattern of the radar. For each of these pulses, the ESM system can measure the amplitude of the pulse, the pulsewidth and the carrier frequency of the RF within the pulse. The system can also measure the time of arrival of the pulse, and, by subtraction of the times of successive pulses from the same emitter, can derive the pulse repetition pattern of the radar. In addition to these characteristics, the system measures the direction of arrival of the pulses. These parameters are shown diagramatically in Figure 3.4, together with a summary of the parameters and a typical resolution to which these parameters are measured.

Many of the parameters could be measured to greater accuracy, but the increased accuracy does not always provide an enhancement to the ESM system, because some of the parameters are corrupted by the varying propagation effects between the radar and the ESM receiver. An example of this is pulsewidth, where multipath propagation produces 'pulse stretching'. Another typical example is the received bearing of the pulse, where, depending on receiver aperture, an accuracy of better than 2 degrees would give a resolution less than the typical dispersion effect which occurs for pulses transmitted across the sea between complex platforms. When a scanning antenna transmits radar pulses across the sea, dispersion effects of typically 8 degrees have been observed due to propagation effects.

A sensitive ESM receiver yields a high rate of received pulses, and this restricts the complexity of the processing that can be applied to every pulse received. The number of sequential processing steps that can be used is limited by the need for a fast response: for

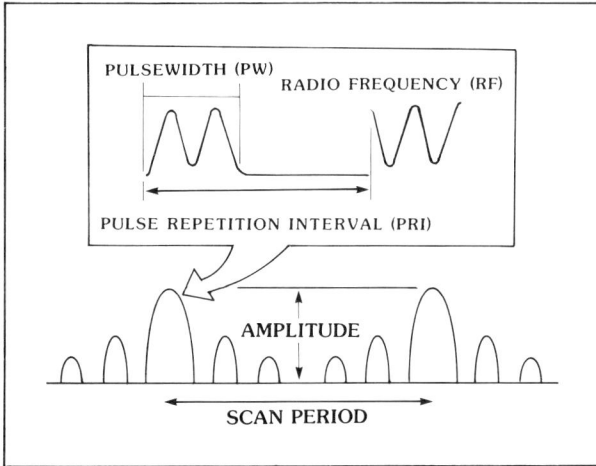

FIG. 3.4   Radar Parameters *(Racal Radar Defence Systems)*

example, the system must give warning of a missile approaching its target early enough for an effective response to be made. The similarity of the radar parameters for different emitters necessitates the use of all available parameters. The system must sort the radars in terms of threat significance, to enable the operator to assimilate the information quickly.

The processing involved consists of three serial stages: (i) sorting of pulses, (ii) segregation of pulse trains and (iii) identification of emitters. Each stage is carried out in parallel for all received emitters, resulting in a system capable of handling high pulse rates and of producing results rapidly with data reduction suitable for human interpretation.

Sorting and segregating pulses from the same emitter again involves three stages: (i) initial sort, (ii) Pulse Repetition Interval (PRI) analysis and (iii) scan analysis. To perform the initial sort, three of the five monopulse parameters, namely true bearing, frequency and pulsewidth, are used in a pigeon-hole de-interleaving scheme. These three are reasonably invariant for non-agile emitters. Time of arrival and amplitude vary from pulse to pulse, and cannot therefore aid the identification of isolated pulses, but they are used for later stages of PRI and scan analysis. The result of the initial sort is the labelling of each pulse received with a cell number, which is used to segregate radar pulses of similar primary parameters into trains.

In Figure 3.5, the segregation of interleaved pulse trains is represented in three dimensions. Suppose a system is receiving the first pulse immediately after switch-on. The angle of arrival, frequency and pulsewidth are measured, and used to define a unique point in three-dimensional space. Now, suppose that a box or cell (Cell 1) is centred on this point having a volume representing the domain of that cell. The next received pulse will either fall into that domain, or outside it. If it falls into the domain of Cell 1, that pulse will be labelled as also belonging to Cell 1, and the domain of Cell 1 will be updated to reflect the centre of the population of pulses belonging to it.

This update of centre of 'mass' of the cell allows the domain of the cell to follow variations in bearing from moving targets and small variations in frequency common in

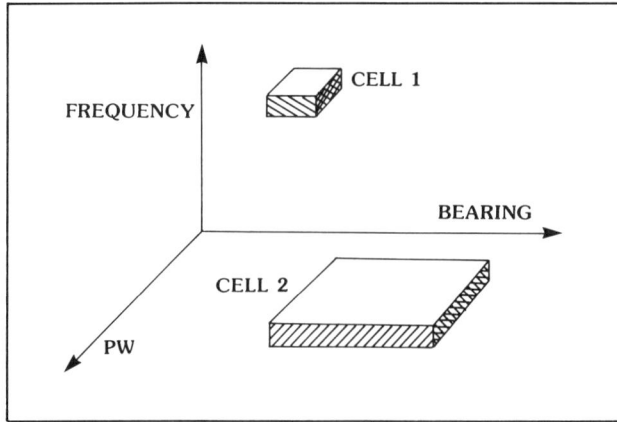

FIG. 3.5   Three-dimensional Representation of Segregation of Interleaved Pulse Trains
(Racal Radar Defence Systems)

navigational radars. Subsequent pulses that do not fall into the domain of Cell 1 create their own cells. Cells are created which cover wide ranges of pulsewidth and bearing but a narrow range of frequencies (Cell 2 in Figure 3.5).

The ensuing de-interleaving by cells is shown in Figure 3.6 where pulses from two interleaved trains have been segregated into separate trains, one for each cell. Just as this spatial segregation aids the eye in determining the pulse repetition pattern of the radar, segregation by cell enables the system to perform the analysis of PRI.

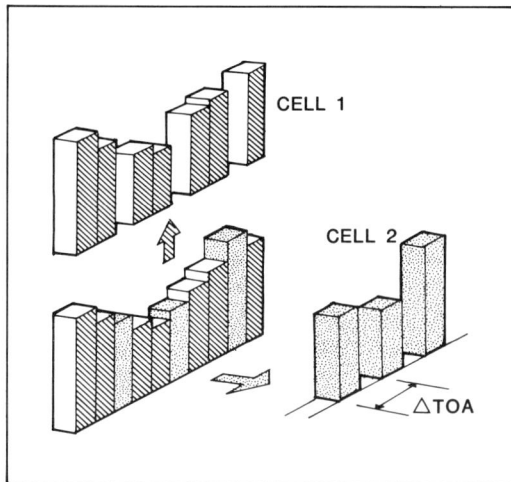

FIG. 3.6   De-interleaving by Cells *(Racal Radar Defence Systems)*

Looking at the pulse train for Cell 2, the pulse interval or difference in time of arrival (TOA) enables a population histogram to be built up for pulse intervals present in the train.

This pulse train (see Figure 3.6) would result in a histogram comprising a single bar at the PRI of the radar. This technique of histogram building is used in the second stage of pulse segregation, in order to enable another parameter, namely time of arrival, to aid emitter de-interleaving. Histograms are built for each cell. Analysis of the population distribution for the histogram enables the value of the emitter's Pulse Repetition Frequency (PRF) and the PRF type (i.e. whether it is a simple pulse train, staggered or jittered) to be determined. Not all radars have simple, regular pulse trains, and hence determining the PRF type is very valuable for emitter identification.

Still more complex pulse trains have characteristic histograms. For example, the pulse train of Cell 1 in Figure 3.6 has two distinct time intervals, resulting from a staggered pulse train, whose histogram consists of two bars, shown on the left of Figure 3.7, whereas jittered pulse intervals result from applying a random variation of 'dither' to a regular pulse train, and give a histogram such as that on the right of Figure 3.7.

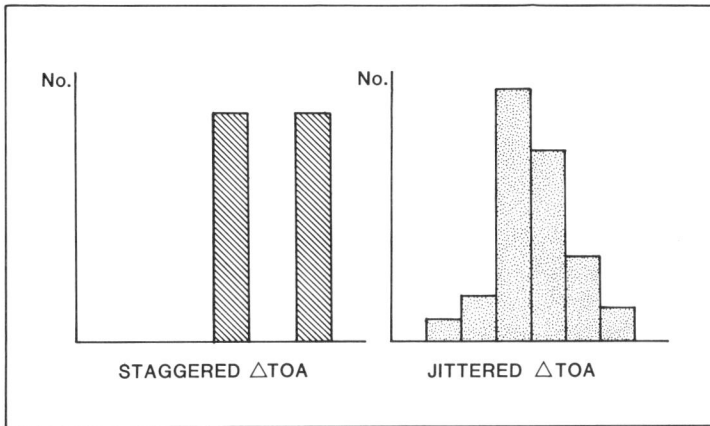

FIG. 3.7   Histograms for Complex Pulse Trains *(Racal Radar Defence Systems)*

Analysing the histograms for each pulse train gives the basic PRF and the PRF type. During this analysis, special care is taken to recognize subharmonics, which result from missing pulses.

In addition to performing PRF analysis, this stage may be thought of as a quality controller on the first stage of pulse de-interleaving. If the histograms formed do not fit any valid PRF type distribution, it can be concluded that the pulse de-interleaving is based on the wrong criteria. This causes the original cell domain to be destroyed and a new one will form.

Successive pulse trains with valid PRF histograms pass on to the next segregation stage, in which amplitude is used to determine longer-term periodicities associated with the scan of the transmitting radar. Here the main difficulty is one of data reduction, as many hundreds of pulses may be received before the scan analysis can be completed for a given cell. The data reduction is achieved by the use of a 'hysteresis peak detector', which reduces the incident pulse stream to a set of pulses which represent the peaks of the waveform. The peak detector produces a single pulse output each time the pulse train for a given cell drops in amplitude by a predetermined hysteresis value after a peak.

The chosen hysteresis level is based on the peak amplitude and the activity ratio for that emitter. The activity ratio is the number of pulses received per second divided by the measured PRF of the source, and is a measure of the percentage illumination of the

ESM receiver by the transmitting antenna. Judicious choice of hysteresis for circular or sector types of scan allows rejection of peaks in the time waveform caused by sidelobes. Emitters with high activity ratio characterise tracking radars illuminating the receiver, and require a low hysteresis value to determine quickly the presence of any modulation indicative of the spatial search pattern of the radar.

This three-stage de-interleaver is implemented as pipelined (i.e. sequential) processing. The first-stage pulse sorting is buffered by a FIFO (first in, first out) buffer on its input and runs at the mean pulse reception rate. The second stage PRI analysis receives data for each pulse, but processes the data in parallel for each pulse train, producing an output per emitter for each scan burst. The third stage uses information on scan bursts together with pulse amplitude to determine the scan pattern of the transmitter, and produces an output about every five scan bursts.

This combination of pipelining and parallelism is the key to success in processing for high emitter pulse density environments. The block diagram in Figure 3.8 represents the integration of the various processing elements to form a system. Initially ignoring the emitter filter, parameter measurement is followed by pulse sorting using pigeon-hole de-interleaving in bearing, pulse-width and frequency, as described previously. This sorting requires extremely fast processing, as the data is in real time and comprises many thousands of pulses per second. The sorted pulse trains pass to the second chronological stage, where PRI histogram analysis, peak detection and averaging are carried out in parallel. Analysis at this second stage is performed simultaneously across data for each cell in the system. These analyses are repeated for each scan burst received.

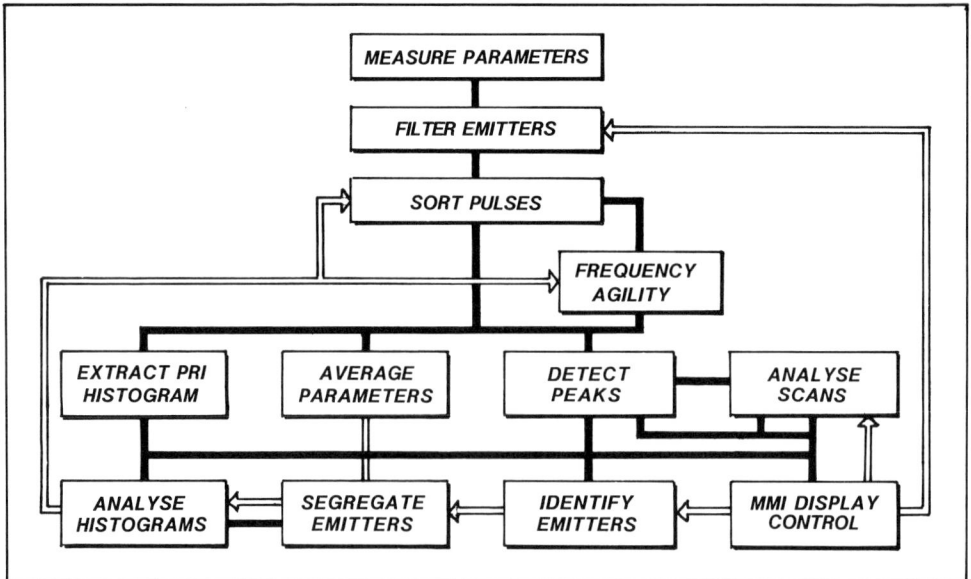

FIG. 3.8   Integration of Various Processing Elements to Form a Complete System
(Racal Radar Defence Systems)

Next, the quality of the PRI histogram is used to measure the success of the pulse sorting in de-interleaving emitters, and to perform adjustment to the pigeon-hole sorter as necessary. Averaging and PRI analyses are performed over the timescales equivalent to an illumination period for surveillance radars or over several hundred pulses for tracking radars. The averaged parameters, including scan periodicity and type, are used to identity emitters by reference to a library of radar parameters, enabling the source of the radar pulses to be identified in less than 1 second from first receipt. In some cases, scan analysis may be required to solve multiple library match problems, and several scan periods must then be received to stabilise the identification. Examination of emitters on the same bearing allows the platform type to be inferred.

The foregoing description only covers emitters for which frequency can be used, with a close tolerance, as a primary de-interleaving parameter. To detect frequency-agile radars, it is necessary to add another layer of processing. The frequency-agile processor uses the output of the sorter, together with a cell's history, to determine whether to process data as constituent pulses from an agile emitter. None of the pulses belonging to an established cell with good PRI analysis are considered candidates for agile processing. Remaining pulses are sorted a second time using a much wider frequency tolerance, which is dynamically updated depending on the frequency distribution of the constituent pulses. Pulses passing through agile cells undergo PRI analysis, averaging and scan analysis in an identical manner to pulses from a fixed-frequency radar. When a radar pulse from a new emitter is first received, the system assumes it is a member of a new fixed as well as a new agile cell. Results from the PRI histogram analysis and the distribution of constituent pulses in the frequency domain are used to decide which hypothesis (agile or fixed) is to be maintained. The other cell is purged to allow its re-use for future emitters.

The man-machine interface (MMI) consists of a display and a keyboard. The ESM display tabulates measured parameters and library identification, as is shown in Figure 3.9. The main table contains one line of information for up to thirty tracks, while columns are included for bearing, frequency, amplitude and library parameters. The track number is used by the operator to interact with the track.

MAIN TRACK DISPLAY   PAGE 1

TRK	BRG	FREQ	AMP	SPOT	CON	FUNC

TRK   023

023   068   16500   6   321332   9.   SRCHH   BRG   068

NEW INPUT   AMP   6

TRK   022   065   2827   3   447619   8,6   ACQEN   PW   1,500

023   FREQ 16500 AGILE 100

022   PRF   2000 FIXED

SCAN   CONSCAN 65

SPOT FUNC CON LIB

1 321332 SRCHH 9 020

2

TOTAL-2   3

4

5

6

HTRK

FIG. 3.9   A Tabular Display *(Racal Radar Defence Systems)*

Inevitably, the need for clarity limits the number of columns that can be presented on a tabular display. Accordingly, many customized formats are used. One format uses a polar plot of inverse signal strength against received bearing. This situation display is particularly useful for detecting emitter movements and clustering. Symbols are used to denote platform type (air, surface, subsurface) and platform threat (hostile/friendly).

In practice, a radar ESM system must perform the following functions:

Cope with nulls caused by multipath lobing.
Recognize emitters with pulses missing through the coincidence of pulses from different emitters.
Analyse emitters exhibiting agility in pulse interval and radio frequency.
Handle signals resulting from reflected as well as direct transmissions.
Handle distortion of pulse width and of amplitude caused by propagation effects.

In practice, the effectiveness of the system is determined by its ability to deal with the problems associated with these effects.

In summary an automatic radar ESM system receives pulses and measures the basic parameters of each pulse. Analysis of frequency, bearing and pulse-width allows de-interleaving into pulse trains, for agile as well as fixed radars. De-interleaving of trains is confirmed by a histogram technique for PRI analysis, which also extracts the PRF and type of the radar.

Peaks in the amplitude distribution of de-interleaved emitters enable scan type and scan period to be determined. All the averaged measured parameters are used to identify the emitters, and groups of emitters on the same bearing allow platforms to be identified. The information is presented to the operator on a variety of visual display formats and as audible signals.

This indicates the method and the degree of complexity involved in ESM signal processing, to achieve signal analysis, and finally to determine the radar identification from which the identity of the platform and the threat it poses may be decided.

DESIGN TRENDS OF CURRENT ESM EQUIPMENT

To realise the tactical advantages which are potentially within the capability of ESM, a range of sophisticated equipment design has evolved in the laboratories of industry. This provides modern navies with a selection of equipments suitable for shipboard use in passive electronic warfare and these are now widely fitted. The performance available, from both hardware and software, is technically impressive but of greater significance is the manner in which engineering design is well matched to the operational requirements and to the way in which the ESM equipments can, most usefully, be employed in the process of naval command and control using electromagnetic sensors. This 'operational suitability' of British naval ESM equipment is rooted in the Royal Navy's concept of the Naval Application Officer employed by equipment designers as an expert user. Serving naval officers carry out this function in Ministry of Defence laboratories, and retired naval officers are employed by industry for the same purpose. As a result, British ESM equipment is particularly effective at sea. Some current ESM equipment designs are discussed below.

One equipment for signal analysis and threat identification which can be used with any ESM system is supplied by Thorn EMI and is known as SARIE (selective automatic radar identification equipment).

In the current radar signal environment, response to a threat must be rapid in order to maintain the safety of the naval vessel or aircraft. This environment will contain a high density of electromagnetic signals which must be detected, analysed, and the degree of threat which they pose evaluated. The SARIE equipment, in service with the Royal Navy and other NATO navies, provides automatic analysis, identification and threat analysis to make possible a rapid response to such situations.

Capable of use with any ESM receiver, the SARIE equipment accepts the video signals derived from intercepted transmissions. Analysis circuits automatically derive signal parameters and other parameters such as frequency, frequency agility and scan can be accepted automatically from the ESM receiver or entered manually. Electronic comparison of the intercepted parameters is made with up to 1000 signatures stored in a programmable library and the results of the comparison are presented on an alpha-numeric display. This display includes information on the signal parameters, possible identification of the signal, the associated platform and a hostility index. Each identification carries a confidence measure figure to enable a priority to be established should the comparison indicate more than one possible identification. Should unknown transmissions be intercepted and analysed, the operator can store this information utilizing a

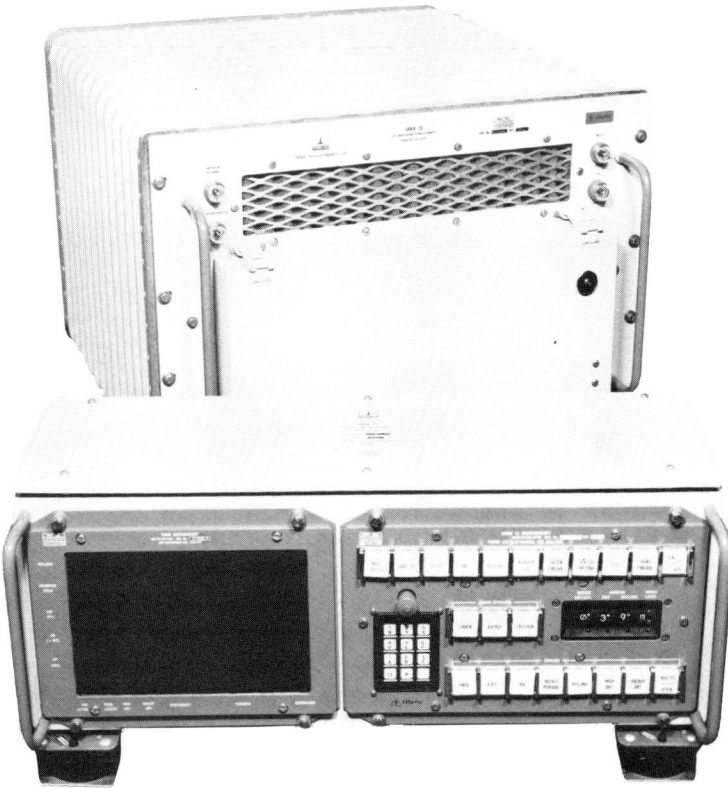

FIG. 3.10   Selective Automatic Radar Identification Equipment (SARIE) *(EMI Electronics)*

built-in scratch pad memory. The new data is then treated as a high priority extension of the library.

The compact modular design of the SARIE equipment makes it suitable for installation in new or existing vessels including fast patrol boats and submarines, aircraft or vehicles.

The SARIE equipment is illustrated in Figure 3.10.

Typical of the sophisticated complete intercept, DF and analysis equipments available for ships from British Industry is the Marconi Defence System's MENTOR.

MENTOR is a low cost, high performance family of ESM systems designed to cover requirements for missile attack warning, surveillance of the radar environment and target acquisition.

Its prime characteristics are a high degree of operational availability, wide frequency coverage, fully software controlled, both automatic and manual control facilities and interfaces to countermeasures.

Built-in test equipment and modular design allows easy fitting to ships without lengthy time out of service. It is easy to maintain and its performance is outlined in the Table below.

Performance Table	Warner	Surveillance	Target Acquisition
Frequency Range GHz	6 to 8	1 to 2	0.5 to 40
Bearing Accuracy	9 degrees	6 degrees	1 degree
Azimuth Coverage	360 degrees	360 degrees	360 degrees
Channels	4	6	6 + Dish aerial
Sensitivity	−45 dBm	−65 dBm	−65 dBm
Dynamic Range	45 dB	55 dB	65 dB
Amplitude Resolution	1 dB	1 dB	1 dB
Radar Store capacity	1000	3000	3000
Processing Time	1 Sec	1 Sec	1 Sec

MENTOR provides a wide range of system configurations and capabilities. The latest advances in technology have been incorporated to provide lightweight equipments including missile warners, surveillance and targeting systems of which the prime features are summarized below.

It provides an unambiguous alarm when the ship is under attack by radar guided missiles. Being fully software controlled allows MENTOR to initiate rapid deployment of offboard countermeasures if required. The surveillance section includes all the warner features plus greater frequency band coverage, enhanced sensitivity, improved DF and greater display capability, thus providing a high performance passive surveillance system which can automatically detect, identify and track a large number of signals simultaneously. Full protection against onboard emissions can also be provided. The target acquisition capability has additional enhancements of even higher sensitivity, further extended frequency coverage to millimetric bands and fine DF. This DF performance enables hostile platforms to be targeted passively.

The main system elements are a masthead unit, a frequency measuring unit and a display console. A modular design of both equipment and software allows flexibility to enable the system to be fitted to a wide range of performance requirements in different classes of ship.

A comprehensive built-in test facilities provides ease of in-service maintenance. A databus interface enables data to be passed to other display stations or ship systems. Automatic warning can be provided to the operator and/or offboard countermeasures of anti-missile attack. MENTOR thus forms a useful part of the ship's defence system.

The masthead assembly can be configured to meet a range of mast types. In general, the assembly includes the DF antennas, RF channels and omni-directional antenna. Masthead assemblies can include four, six or eight channels, depending upon requirement. A key feature of the design is the capability to extend the system to millimetric wavelengths. Suitable filter sub-units can be provided to overcome onboard system interference.

MENTOR ESM consoles can be provided in a range of sizes and shapes ergonomically designed to meet installation requirements in different ships. Included in the console are comprehensive signal processing units, dual video display units having multiple display formats, operator controls, recording facilities and in-built power supplies. The system identifies a range of radar types and modes enabling the operator to keep track of a number of intercepted emitters.

A range of tabular and activity displays are at the finger tip control of the operator. This allows him to monitor emission activity, investigate intercepted parameters, and track hostile emissions. A data manipulation display is also provided to enable the operator to amend, add or delete data held in the library or warner files.

The Frequency Measuring Unit is compact and can be installed either in the masthead assembly or at the foot of the mast. The equipment is illustrated in diagram form in Figure 3.11 and the physical appearance of the office console is shown in Figure 3.12.

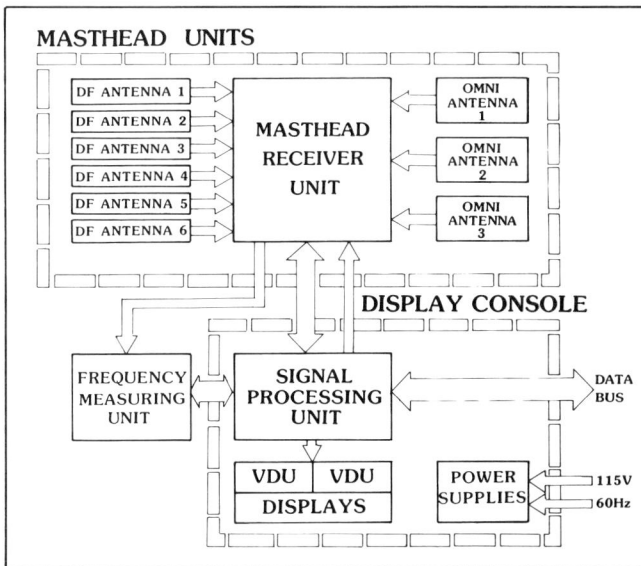

FIG. 3.11   The MENTOR System *(Marconi Defence Systems)*

CO $_2$ INJECTION NOZZLE

SPACE FOR
ECM PANEL

VCS ALARM
UNIT

VDU

VDU

CASSETTE/DISK
PLAYER/RECORDER

THERMAL PRINTER

STALK LIGHT

TRACKER BALL

VCS COMMS
UNIT

MICROPHONE/
HEADPHONES

KEYBOARD

DOOR(ELECTRONIC ACCESS)

CONSOLE

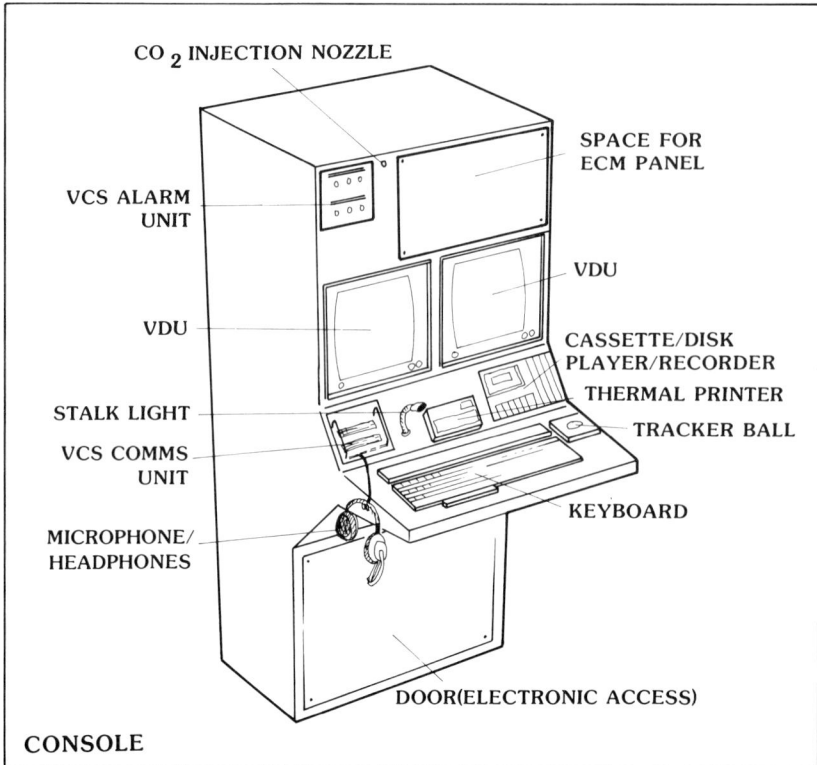

FIG. 3.12   MENTOR Operator's Console *(Marconi Defence Systems)*

Warnings of Laser Illumination

A warning of illumination by a laser beam is tactically useful since some weapons are now guided by laser beam reflections from a target. The laser warning receiver gives a response and indicates the presence and approximate direction of laser signals from rangefinders, target designators and beam-riding missile guidance sources. Even a single pulse can be detected and recognized, and as a consequence appropriate countermeasures can be taken to improve the survivability of the ship, boat or helicopter. Usually the direction of the threat is given to within a 45 degree sector and an audible warning is initiated. A determination of the laser wavelength to within 100 nm may be provided to assist in threat identification, and the signal strength may be assessed. A wide spectrum coverage from 350 to 1100 nm is normally available together with an angular coverage of 360 degrees in azimuth.

The Marconi Company provide such an equipment which is representative of the extent to which electronic warfare now embraces electro-optical sensors and systems which are used for weapon direction and guidance. This type of ESM is more relevant to the protection of helicopters and small naval vessels which are more frequently the targets of laser-guided weapons at short range than are larger ships. The same type of equipment is also, of course, very relevant to the protection of Army vehicles. The design is compact and the total weight is typically some six kilogrammes.

The basic direction finding system consists of three modules: a small head unit, which is externally mounted in a position providing an unobscured field of view, the electronics unit which is mounted remotely at a convenient place within the vehicle, and a control and display unit. An optional extension of the basic system allows determination of laser wavelengths, received signal strength, and more detailed threat characterization. For trials purposes, this module incorporates a raw data display panel (showing signal strength in each wavelength channel); a simple processor can, however, show reduced data in terms of peak threat wavelength, power, and likely threat classification or identification.

Calibration

Facilities are necessary for the calibration and maintenance of ESM equipment. CALFAC is a shore based system for the calibration and monitoring of the performance of EW systems installed in naval vessels and helicopters. Utilising software controlled system management for the generation and reception of signals and their recording and analysis, rapid accurate calibration of radar ESM and ECM systems is achieved. To calibrate ESM systems, radar type reference signals are transmitted at accurately defined frequencies, pulse widths and pulse repetition frequencies. The overall accuracy of the DF portion of the ESM system under calibration is checked by comparison with an independent DF reference system utilising acoustic, hyperbolic radio or transponder techniques and operated in conjunction with the CALFAC system. The performance of ECM equipment is assessed by analysing the jamming signals transmitted by the equipment under test in response to test signals generated by the CALFAC system.

A modular construction has been adopted for the CALFAC sub systems which are housed in transportable containers and the overall system is capable of relocation to a new site, if required, where it can provide a range of facilities from performance checking to complete calibration.

CALFAC is provided by Thorn EMI and is representative of the facilities needed to support the sophisticated ESM systems now being fitted in ships and aircraft.

ESM Equipments for Major Warships

For major warships, the CUTLASS equipment (produced by Racal Radar Defence Systems Ltd) is representative of the sophistication in design and performance of present day ESM.

The CUTLASS B1 equipment is an automatic ESM system designed to operate in a dense radar environment. It receives signals in the 2–18GHz frequency range, measures their parameters and compares these with a pre-programmed radar library. The ESM Operator is then presented with both tabular and graphic displays of signal identity, bearing and threat significance.

The equipment employs a receiver and antenna system to intercept RF signals in its operational frequency range. The bearing is measured using a unique thirty-two element array which provides an instantaneous 360 degrees coverage with an exceptionally high bearing accuracy.

The high pulse density of up to several hundreds of thousand pulses per second expected in a modern naval environment presents a formidable task for the system processor. To meet this requirement a special purpose, high speed processing system is incorporated.

Selected data on threats received can be routed automatically, under simple operator command, to the Action Information Organization (AIO) and Electronic Countermeasures (ECM) system as required.

A magnetic tape unit is provided for emitter scenario recording and playback purposes. This can also be used to record new library entries created during the mission using the 100 entry auxiliary library function. In addition, a printer is provided to record intercept data which may subsequently be used for post mission and intelligence analysis.

The system divides into two major parts: the ESM receiver and the ESM signal processor:

The ESM receiver spans the frequency range 2 to 18GHz and uses two digital bearing and frequency discriminators over 2 to 7.5GHz and 7.5 to 18GHz. These units provide an instantaneous measurement of bearing and frequency and pass digitized pulse data to the signal processor in real time.

The ESM signal processor accepts the outputs from the ESM Receiver and by means of a combination of special purpose circuits and a digital data processor, de-interleaves the overlapping pulse trains from different radars and measures additional parameters of each radar such as scan type and scan period. The processor then makes the most likely identification of radars by comparison with the pre-programmed library and information about the radar signal environment is presented to the operator on an ordered, tabular display and on a graphic situation display.

The antenna for each band consists of a circular array of thirty-two slot line radiator elements equi-spaced in azimuth. Each element is connected to an input port of a BUTLER MATRIX. When a signal is received the phase differences between the output ports and a reference port are directly related to the bearing of the received signal.

The ESM Receiver consists of two digital bearing and frequency discriminators, covering 2 to 7.5 GHz and 7.5 to 18 GHz, together with additional circuitry for control logic and data selectors to allow interfacing with the ESM processor. Each unit accepts the appropriate, amplified RF signal from the antenna and feed matrix output ports.

When a signal is received, the digital bearing discriminator of the appropriate band compares the phase difference between the reference channel and the output ports to determine an accurate and unambiguous bearing of the source of the received signal.

The frequency of incoming signals is measured by means of an instantaneous digital frequency discriminator. The bearing and frequency discriminators have a high dynamic range and so do not require switchable attenuators. The video amplifiers used are DC coupled and allow the system to respond to CW signals.

The emitter list in the radar library may consist of up to 2000 entries, each of which may specify an emitter or an emitter mode. Each entry consists of the following parameters:

> Carrier Frequency (Min/Max)
> Carrier Frequency Agility
> Pulse Width (Min/Max)
> PRF (Min/Max)

PRF Modulation Type (fixed, jitter etc)
PRF Modulation Parameter
Scan Type
Scan Period (Min/Max)
Identity
Confidence Level
Function
ECM Response Mode
Platform

Permanent storage of library data is on magnetic type cartridges. On system initialization, the library is loaded by the operator into the system semi-conductor RAM memory.

The input to the library identification program is the output of the signal processor. Its outputs are:

Identification
Threat Priority
Confidence Level

These outputs are achieved by comparing the input parameters with a store of radar types and their parameters. The degree of 'fit' with which the parameters coincide contributes to the probability that it is a correct identification or, in other words, the confidence level.

The method of identification is essentially a decoding operation relating input measured values to output radar types and probabilities. Identification decisions are based on the relative importance of the radar parameters so that the speed of identification is optimized. Identification decisions are made on the individual radar's parameters and a final identification and probability assessment is computed by combining the individual decisions assuming that each decision is independent of any other decision.

The library of emitter data is initially loaded into the store from a magnetic tape reader. Thereafter identification is made at high speed using the store with no further reference to the tape. The library data used for identification is prepared from intelligence data and a magnetic cartridge that contains the library data is produced. The library tape so obtained contains the parameter tolerances and takes into consideration the different modes of a particular emitter type.

Information about the radar environment is presented to the operator in two forms; as a tabular display and a graphic display. The system displays are generated by table driven software and are therefore readily adaptable to meet specific requirements.

The main tabular display area shown in Figure 3.13 presents information on up to twenty-five radars organized under track number and ordered in decreasing severity of the threat. Normally, details of the twenty-five most serious threats are displayed automatically, but information on up to 150 intercepts can be displayed in six pages of twenty-five under operator control. Significant changes in the threat situation are indicated to the operator even if he has selected pages other than that displaying the highest priority intercepts.

EW—D

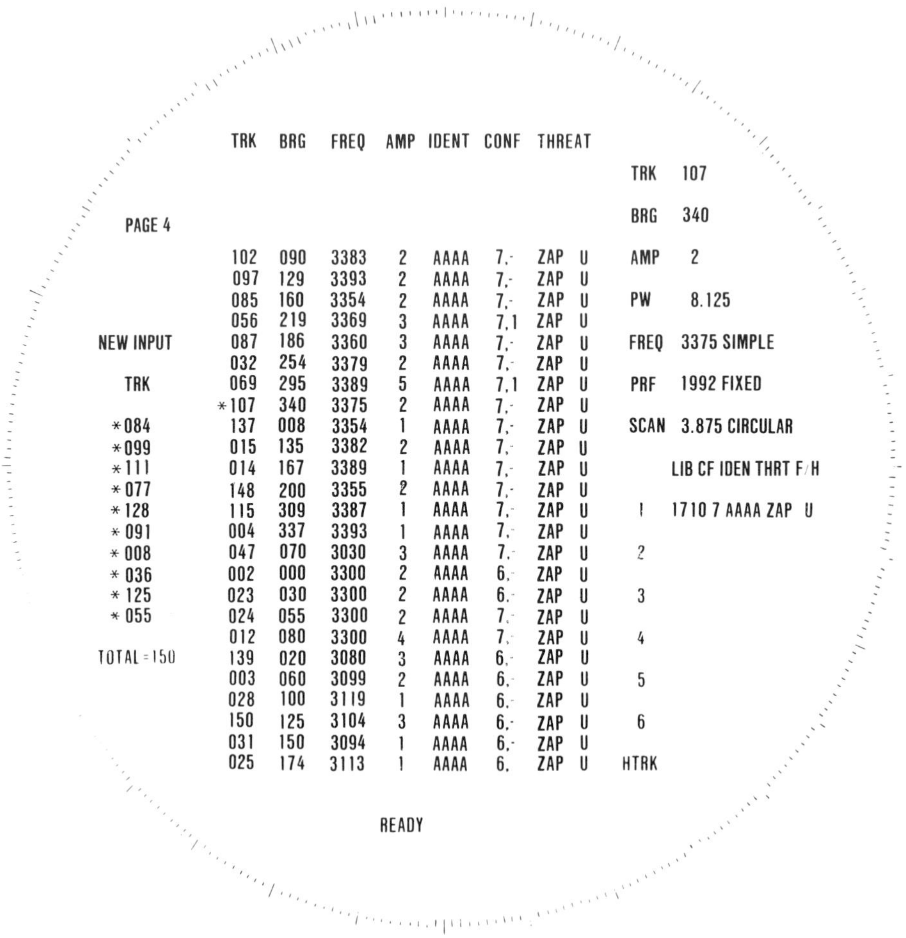

	TRK	BRG	FREQ	AMP	IDENT	CONF	THREAT			
									TRK	107
									BRG	340
PAGE 4										
	102	090	3383	2	AAAA	7.-	ZAP	U	AMP	2
	097	129	3393	2	AAAA	7.-	ZAP	U		
	085	160	3354	2	AAAA	7.-	ZAP	U	PW	8.125
	056	219	3369	3	AAAA	7.1	ZAP	U		
NEW INPUT	087	186	3360	3	AAAA	7.-	ZAP	U	FREQ	3375 SIMPLE
	032	254	3379	2	AAAA	7.-	ZAP	U		
TRK	069	295	3389	5	AAAA	7.1	ZAP	U	PRF	1992 FIXED
	*107	340	3375	2	AAAA	7.-	ZAP	U		
*084	137	008	3354	1	AAAA	7.-	ZAP	U	SCAN	3.875 CIRCULAR
*099	015	135	3382	2	AAAA	7.-	ZAP	U		
*111	014	167	3389	1	AAAA	7.-	ZAP	U		LIB CF IDEN THRT F/H
*077	148	200	3355	2	AAAA	7.-	ZAP	U		
*128	115	309	3387	1	AAAA	7.-	ZAP	U	1	1710 7 AAAA ZAP U
*091	004	337	3393	1	AAAA	7.-	ZAP	U		
*008	047	070	3030	3	AAAA	7.-	ZAP	U	2	
*036	002	000	3300	2	AAAA	6.-	ZAP	U		
*125	023	030	3300	2	AAAA	6.-	ZAP	U	3	
*055	024	055	3300	2	AAAA	7.-	ZAP	U		
	012	080	3300	4	AAAA	7.-	ZAP	U	4	
TOTAL=150	139	020	3080	3	AAAA	6.-	ZAP	U		
	003	060	3099	2	AAAA	6.-	ZAP	U	5	
	028	100	3119	1	AAAA	6.-	ZAP	U		
	150	125	3104	3	AAAA	6.-	ZAP	U	6	
	031	150	3094	1	AAAA	6.-	ZAP	U		
	025	174	3113	1	AAAA	6.	ZAP	U	HTRK	

READY

FIG. 3.13   CUTLASS Tabular Display *(Racal Radar Defence Systems)*

The information displayed is:

Track Number
Bearing
Radio Frequency
Amplitude
Most Likely Identification
Confidence Level
Confidence Level of next most likely identification
Threat Type

Tracks are updated as soon as new information is available but no faster than at one second intervals.

The right-hand side of the display presents more detailed information about any particular radar that has been selected by the operator.

The main table entry is marked with an asterisk alongside the track number.

The more detailed information displayed is:

Track Number
Bearing
Radio Frequency
Radio Frequency Agility
Amplitude
Six most likely Identifications with Confidence Levels
Pulse Width
Pulse Repetition Frequency
Pulse Repetition Frequency Agility
Scan Type
Scan Period

The tabular display normally shows tracks in order of threat priority with the top five track lines blank. When new threat tracks are displayed, whichever page is being viewed, they are put into these blank spaces. High priority threats may be indicated with flashing asterisk alongside the THREAT TYPE of the track concerned. The operator may initiate re-assembly of the page into threat order by the use of the keyboard and the top five lines will then again be blank.

When new emitters are intercepted, a table on the extreme left of the display indicates all the new tracks by their track number. The operator may select any of these new tracks for detailed display on the right-hand side without changing page.

At the bottom of the display is a read-back of the operator's keyboard entries so that he knows what stage has been reached in a command sequence. Above this is a space for messages from the system to the operator in the form of prompts or indications of errors in keying.

The operator may select an alternative display format, normally provided as standard. This is similar to the main tabular display with the addition of scan and PRF information in place of library identification details. Other secondary display formats are also possible.

The graphic display is illustrated in Figure 3.14 and consists of four sections.

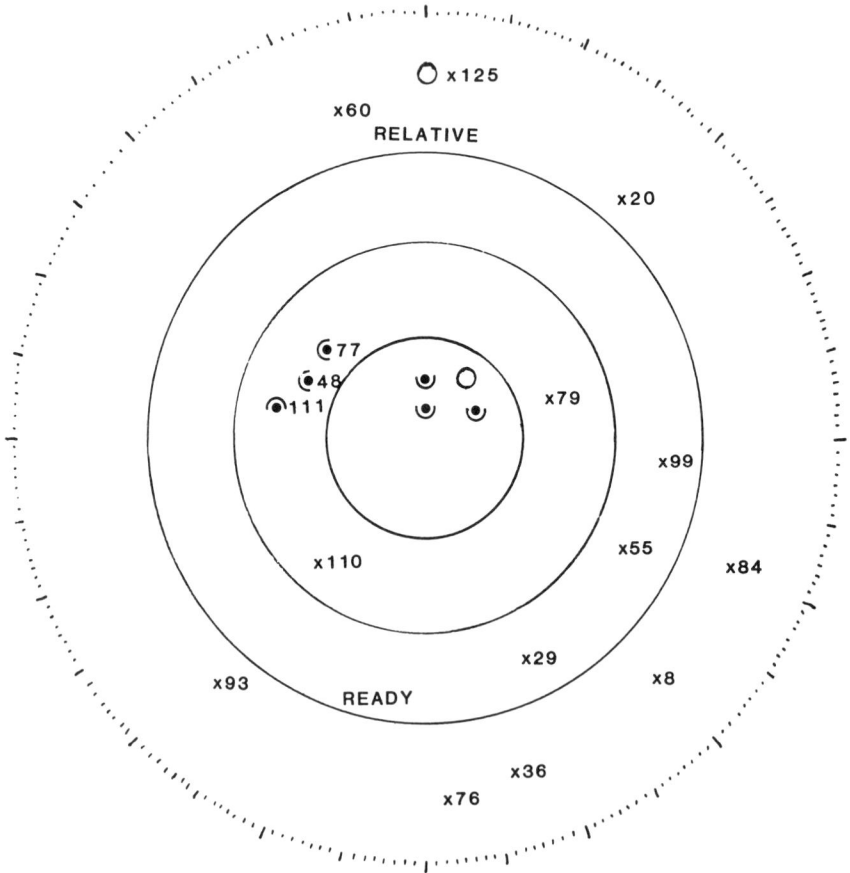

FIG. 3.14   CUTLASS Graphic Display *(Racal Radar Defence Systems)*

   (i) The inner section shows the bearing of friendly signals relative to true North. The distance from the centre of the display is inversely proportional to the signal strength. The type of radar platform is indicated by standard symbols as shown.

   (ii) The second section indicates the bearing and inverse amplitude of neutral radars. The type of radar platform is indicated by standard symbols.

  (iii) The third section indicates the bearing and inverse amplitude of all known hostile radars. Each radar has its relevant track number displayed as well as the symbol. All radars have their two previous positions on the display indicated by a dot.

  (iv) The outer section contains remaining unknown signals. Each radar is indicated by the appropriate symbol and track number. Bearing and amplitude are indicated as in the other sections.

The total number of radars displayed in each section does not exceed 20. These are automatically chosen as the highest priority emissions in each section.

The complete operators console is shown in Figure 3.15.

CANEWS, provided by the MEL company, is a comparable ESM system for major warships. It is a sensitive and accurate early warning system with a complete signal processing capability for the identification of intercepted radar signals. It uses amplitude-comparison direction finding and instantaneous frequency measurement and has a 100 per cent intercept probability; it can be integrated into a ship's sensor and command system by a data bus.

One operator only is required to control the complete ESM system. Data is processed automatically and clearly displayed in a number of different information formats. There is however a manual pulse analyser which enables an operator to undertake additional complex analysis. The operator can also expand a selected frequency band in order to interrogate dense parts of the spectrum more closely.

The CANEWS ESM system consists of six items of equipment:

    Frequency-Antenna Assembly
    Masthead Direction Finding Assembly
    Masthead Built-in Test Equipment (BITE) Assembly
    Receiver Cabinet Assembly
    Analyser Cabinet
    Operators Display Console

The display console has a high resolution colour display to assist in differentiating between friendly and hostile signals and the real-time frequency/bearing presentation of signals can show 'raw' and synthetic data. As well as an automatic pulse analyser there is the manual analyser to enable an operator to carry out detailed analysis of new or complex signals. A rollerball and control panel enables part of the display to be expanded where the signals are dense, and provides an interface with the ship's command system and ECM equipments. Information can be recorded for later analysis and there is an extensive memory capacity for the library of signatures used in recognition. The aerial units are shown in Figure 3.16.

CANEWS is a major ESM system which provides all the range of sophisticated facilities to analyse the signal environment which are now required in large ships. It requires an experienced and trained operator to obtain full advantage from its quite complex facilities but it represents the upper level of ESM capability in equipment

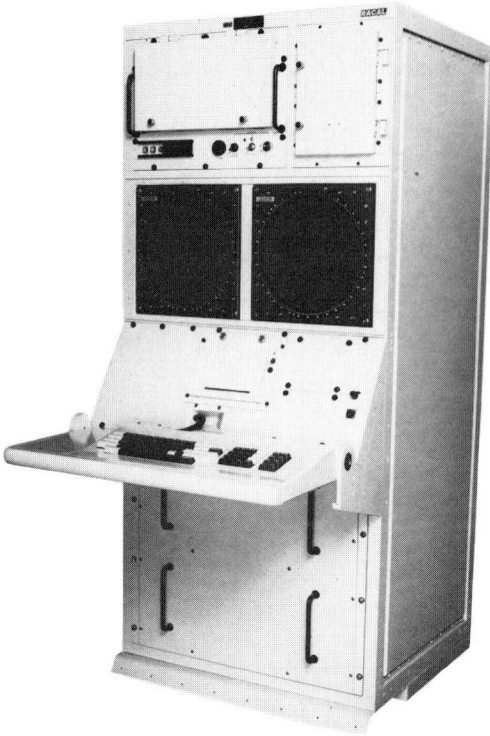

FIG. 3.15   CUTLASS Operator's Console and the Complete Equipment Fitted on an Egyptian RAMADAN Class Patrol Craft *(Racal Radar Defence Systems)*

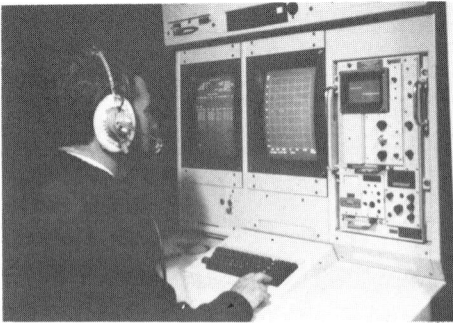

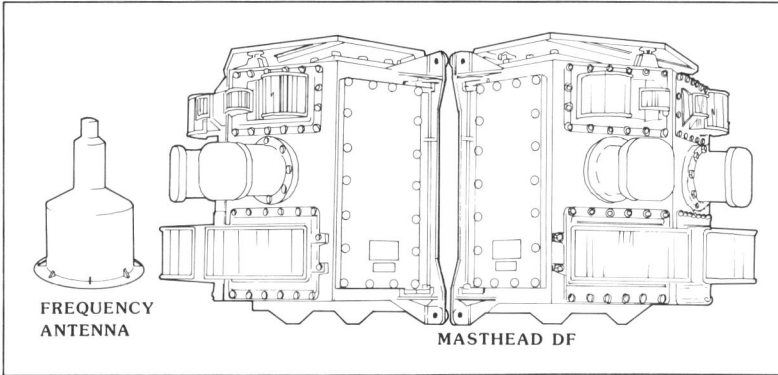

FIG. 3.16 The CANEWS ESM Aerials *(MEL)*

currently available. A very great deal of valuable tactical information can be obtained from equipment of this type and its sophistication pays a rich dividend in naval operations.

ESM Equipment for Submarines

For submarines, the Racal PORPOISE ESM equipment is an excellent example of this class of modern EW capability.

The system divides into three major parts:

The Antenna Assembly
The ESM Digitizer Unit
The Operator's Console

These are shown in Figure 3.17.

The Antenna Assembly covers the frequency range 2–18 GHz in two bands 2–8GHz and 8–18GHz. For each band there is an omni antenna for frequency measurement and a 6 port array for bearing measurement. Spiral antennas form the array for the low band and waveguide horns are used for the high band array. Amplification and signal conditioning of antenna outputs are carried out within the antenna assembly. A built-in-test facility is fitted which enables RF signals to be injected at the inputs of the antennas. The outputs of the antenna assembly are RF signals for frequency, and video signals for bearing measurement.

Antenna sub-assemblies have been designed to enable replacement as complete pre-tested and calibrated units. The antenna assembly and ESM mast interface is a high corrosion resistant casting with tapered sides designed to reduce the radar echoing area; in addition the faces are coated with a radar absorbing material suitable for underwater use. The radome is manufactured from high quality glass re-inforced plastic with low water absorption properties.

The ESM Digitizer Unit is located within the hull but as close to the ESM mast as possible to minimize RF feeder losses. It receives the RF and video signals from the

Antenna
Array
Exterior,
showing
Radome

Interior, showing
construction in Titanium
to reduce weight

ESM Digitizer
Unit

Operator's
Console

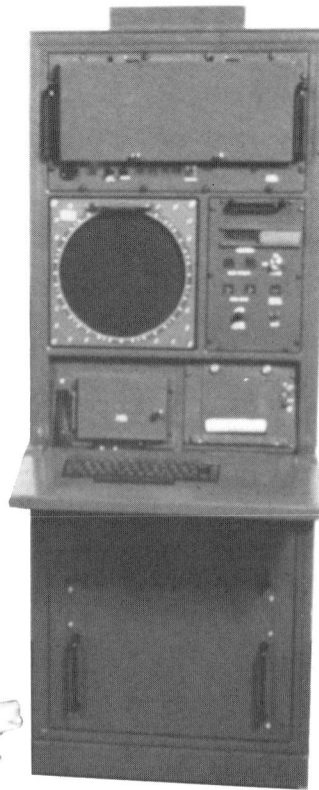

FIG. 3.17   PORPOISE Submarine ESM Equipment (Racal Radar Defence Systems)

Antenna Assembly and outputs digital words. Bearing is derived by comparing the amplitude of signals received by adjacent DF antennas with correction applied for systematic errors. Amplitude is also measured from these antenna but is corrected to allow for the beam pattern using the measured bearing. Frequency is measured via the omni-directional antennas using digital instantaneous frequency measurement techniques.

The outputs of the bearing, amplitude, pulse width, time of arrival and frequency measurement circuits are combined to form a single word. When completed the word is passed to the processors in the operator's console for analysis.

The Operator's Console. The signal processor receives digital signals from the ESM digitizer unit and de-interleaves the pulse trains of the different radars to derive the parameters including scan period for each radar. The processor then makes the most likely identification of the received radars by comparison with a pre-programmed library. The resultant information about the radar signal environment is then presented to the operator on the display.

The alpha numeric keyboard allows the operator to select a radar for detailed display of its parameters or to display the parameters of any known radars held in the memory. In addition the keyboard permits the operator to inject selected digital data to the ship's data systems and also to select audio on a frequency band or track basis.

The display can be selected by the operator to present radar signal environment data either in an ordered tabular format or in a graphic format. In the tabular format up to 25 radar tracks from the signal processor tracking store of 150 tracks can be displayed at any one time.

Tracks are displayed in threat priority order and any radar identified as a high priority threat triggers an audible alarm and a flashing asterisk is shown against the 'threat type' on the display. The alarm may be cancelled using the keyboard. In the graphic format the display is divided into four annular rings which display friendly, neutral, hostile and unknown radars up to a maximum of 20 radars per classification.

The library tape contains data on radar emitter signatures including the classification of an emitter into friendly, or hostile. The system library has a capacity of 2000 emitter modes of which 1960 are inserted via the library tape and the remaining 40 modes are available for the operator to create a subsidiary library.

A printer enables the operator to obtain a hard copy of radar parameters selected from the tabular display. Automatic fault finding using the BITE facility is controlled by the processor. The test programme used will enable location of a fault to printed circuit board level.

The MEL MANTA system is another very good example of ESM equipment for submarine operations. For submarines it provides ESM coverage from 2 to 18 GHz with 100 per cent interrupt probability, an automatic threat warner which can recognise 144 radar signals and a comprehensive signal analysis capability. It provides a periscope aerial and a more comprehensive DF aerial on a separate mast giving bearing accuracy of some 6 degrees RMS.

The operators console is shown in Figure 3.18 and the complete equipment outline in Figure 3.19. This equipment is typical of the sophisticated, software-based form of modern ESM at sea today and is indicative of the tactical value provided by EW in submarine operations.

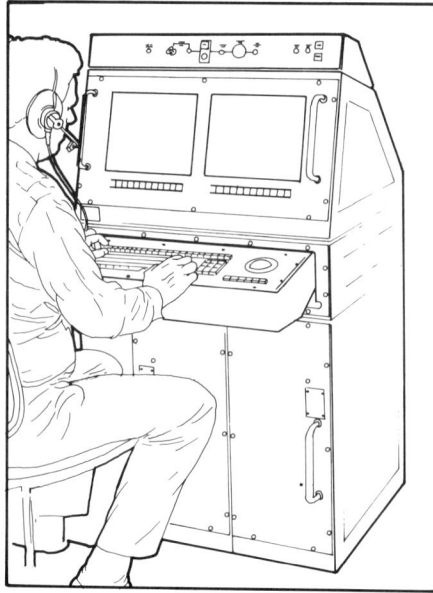

FIG. 3.18   MANTA Submarine ESM Operator's Console *(MEL)*

ESM Equipment for Small Surface Ships

For small surface ships the Racal SEA SAVIOUR is an interesting example of EW equipment designed to match accurately the operational need of this class of vessel. Modern weaponry and missile systems make it necessary for even the smallest of vessels (FPBs, MCMVs etc.) and support ships to have a minimum EW capability. The case is stronger still for vessels not able to use firepower as a means of defending themselves and having to rely solely on alternative methods.

SEA SAVIOR is a simple cost-effective solution to today's requirement of enhancing a vessel's survivability. The system is capable of immediate recognition of hostile radar threats and couples this with optional automatic countermeasure reaction, such as chaff deployment, to provide a fast reaction system.

The SEA SAVIOUR system reduces vulnerability to radar associated threats at sea by providing the Command with a timely and unambiguous threat warning. This permits the appropriate countermeasures, usually manoeuvre and chaff discharge, to be effectively and rapidly employed. System design has taken account of the likely need to integrate frequency extensions in order to enhance further the survivability of the vessel. The system has a high probability of intercept and a low false alarm rate.

By means of a processor and using programmable threat data on defined threats, the warner automatically alerts the Command to the presence of these imminent threats, and gives an indication of bearing. A facility to interface with a chaff dispensing system is available to provide a fully automatic countermeasure.

A four-port antenna system is employed which provides RF for bearing and frequency measurement. The processor is designed to extract the data necessary to recognise the presence of real threats with a high degree of confidence. Threat presence is indicated on

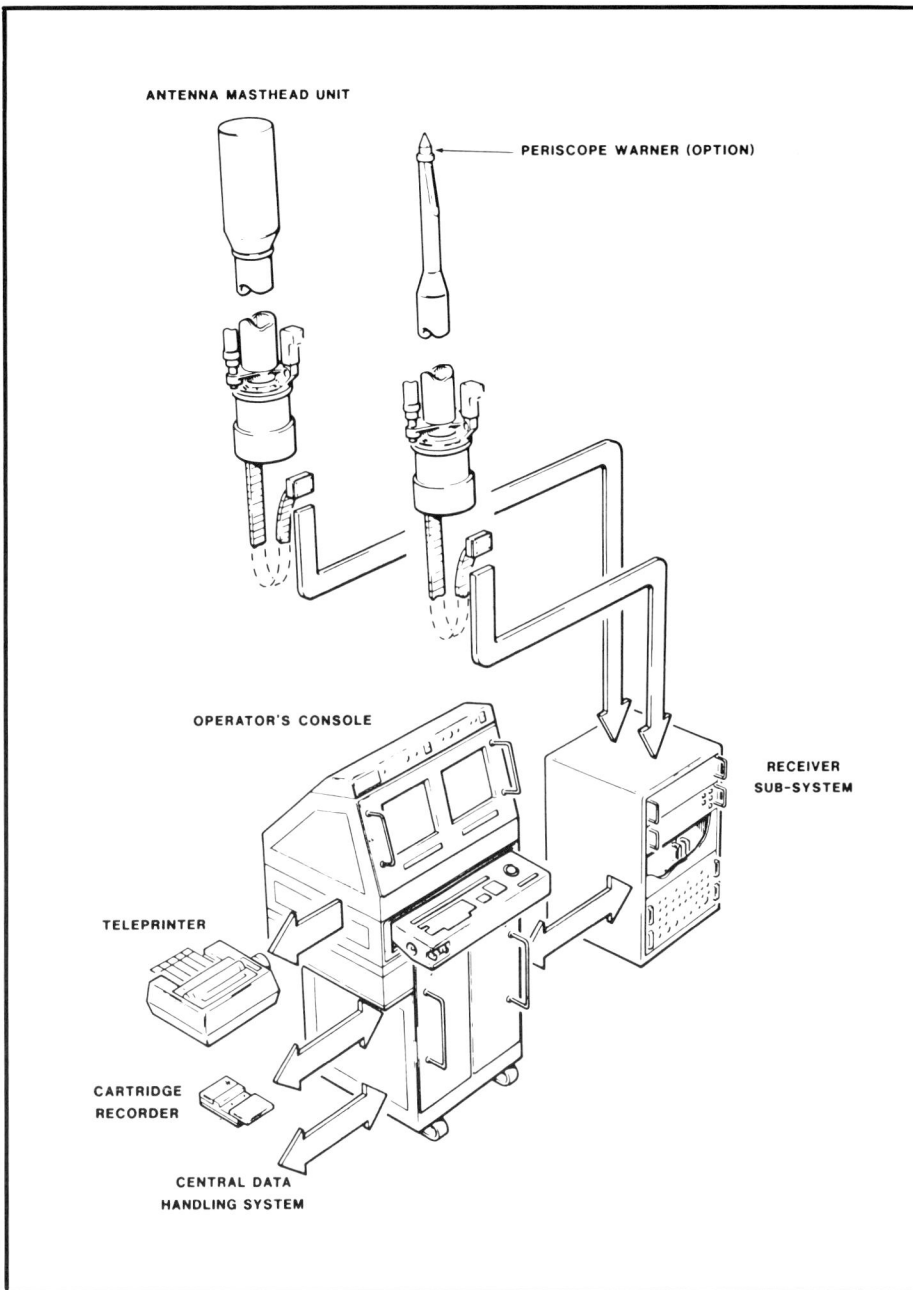

FIG. 3.19   MANTA Layout *(MEL)*

both a display and by the sounding of an audible warning device at suitable locations as required within the vessel. SEA SAVIOUR is easily reprogrammed at sea.

The display uses light emitting diodes and up to three threats can be displayed simultaneously. The information displayed for each threat is an arrow giving the direction of the threat relative to ship's heading with octangle resolution, together with a three character alphanumeric identifier.

Operating over the frequency range 6 to 18 GHz the system measures and digitizes the frequency, amplitude and pulse width of each intercepted radar pulse and examines the pulse-by-pulse data to determine whether it matches the characteristics of known threats stored in a library held in the data processor. For non-threat emissions the data is discarded but where threat characteristics are observed, further processing is carried out to determine the mean PRF of the emitter. If this also matches a threat, then the display is activated and an audible alarm is generated.

Amplitude comparison techniques are used to compute the bearing of the threat emitters. A non-volatile solid-state memory is used to store the defined threat data which is re-programmable at sea. Up to sixty-four threat emitter signatures can be stored. Provision is made for the expansion of library capacity.

This system can be expanded to cover other frequency bands and the storage of additional threat emitters in these frequency bands. The basic equipment comprises the following:

> A wrap around masthead unit containing four antenna units and one frequency measuring receiver.
> A data processor and power supply unit.
> A display and control unit.
> Up to 2 displays can be driven simultaneously if required and a speech synthesis unit is available to give verbal indication of threat direction and identification.

For smaller surface ships without specialist EW operators there is a particular ESM equipment provided by MEL known as RAPIDS which uses a high degree of automation designed to make it as self-contained and as operator-independent as possible. It would not provide as full or complete an analysis of the signal environment as, for example, CANEWS, but it is complex to a high degree in the method of its operation.

Despite their relatively small size and high speed, Fast Patrol Boats (FPBs) are still a target for air or surface launched anti-ship missiles. Without prior warning of the existence of an enemy vessel of aircraft, there is little chance of detecting an incoming missile before it is too late to initiate counter-measures, or to attempt evasive manoeuvres.

RAPIDS is a compact, lightweight radar intercept ESM system that detects threats at long range. The system features fully automatic threat and lock-on warners so that continuous manning is not required—an obvious benefit in space-restricted small craft where crew levels must be reduced to a minimum. Operator intervention and manual operation are also possible via the electronic data display console. This ability to operate as a stand-alone system could be crucial in the event of damage to the ship's surveillance radar or the Action Information Organisation (AIO)—or Operations Room.

RAPIDS uses wide-open 360 degree ESM technology which intercepts and classifies radar emitters faster than a scanning system. In addition RAPIDS detects every target within range; a scanning system can sometimes fail to detect a short radar emission made in the non-scanned area during its rotation period.

RAPIDS can operate as a 'stand-alone' unit or can be fully integrated with the Ships Tactical Data Handling System and ECM system.

The main features of the system are as follows:

(a)   An antenna system covering the range 2–18 GHz and having all round cover through 360 degrees and good elevation cover up to 50 degrees with 2 degrees bearing accuracy. It is essential in the naval scenario to have continuous all round cover in azimuth, because it may often be necessary to detect short bursts of transmission. Such short bursts may come from an aircraft search radar energised for just two or three sweeps or from a submarine ranging radar. This means that the antenna needs to be a multi-port device rather than a rotating dish.

(b)   A receiver of high sensitivity and continuous cover over the whole frequency band with 100 per cent probability of detection. A receiver which sweeps or steps through the frequency band is not appropriate because of the need again to detect short burst of transmitted energy. The receiver measures the following parameters to a high degree of accuracy:

      Bearing
      Frequency
      Amplitude
      Pulse Width
      Time of Arrival

(c)   These parameters can then be fed, usually in digital form, to the processor sub-system. The processor has the task of sorting a multiplicity of signals into identifiable radar signals. This process is known as de-interleaving and has been discussed earlier. The de-interleaved information is then further processed to give all the radar parameters for each radar which are:

      Bearing
      Frequency
      Amplitude
      Pulse Width
      PRI or PRF
      Scan rate

Having obtained these parameters they are compared with a library of information such that each radar can be identified.

(d)   In RAPIDS the display system depicts radar frequency against bearing (real time data) and alpha numeric information on particular radars. The control of the system is by soft keys and a light pen; the soft keys are part of the display panel.

Detection of Weapon Radars

Specifically for detection and warning of a locked-on missile or gun fire control radar is the MEL Company's MATILDA which stands for Microwave Analysis, Threat

Indication and Launch Detection Apparatus. MATILDA provides the Command with an automatic alarm the moment an enemy tracking radar illuminates or locks-on to the vessel. The command can then take immediate action to protect the vessel. MATILDA however also eliminates any human time delay which may occur by triggering a chaff decoy system, initiating the point-defence weapon system, switching tracking radars into a search mode or by activating a radar-jamming system such as SCIMITAR. If required, it initiates other defensive actions by interfacing with the ship's Action Data Computer.

MATILDA shows the success of the counter measures by reverting to its normal passive state within two seconds of the threat being eliminated—i.e. the disengagement of the locked-on enemy radar. It is primarily intended for ships carrying no ESM equipment but it also performs an essential role in ships fitted with older, manual ESM systems.

The MATILDA system consists of a four port aerial array, a control unit containing a specialised micro-computer and a sector display unit. The sector display unit will give a visual indication of the sector within which the attack is developing. In addition there is a synthesised voice alarm giving an alert on the required sector. For example 'Alert, Alert, Green 45'. The sector display may be in the Operations Room and may be duplicated on the Bridge. The voice alarm may also be linked into the ship's Action Information Broadcast or the ships Main Broadcast. MATILDA will give this alert within one second of a 'locked on' signal being detected.

The alarm will give at least thirty seconds warning of a missile's approach. Even if nothing else were done this would give the command and crew sufficient time to take evasive action and to brace themselves for a possible missile hit or near miss.

MATILDA is an effective, low-cost, fit-and-forget system to protect vessels from the threat of air or surface-launched missiles. Its low initial cost, minimal operating and maintenance requirements and compact size make it eminently suitable for Mine Counter-Measure Vessels, Logistic Support Ships, Corvettes, Frigates, Fast Patrol Boats, Hydrofoils and Hovercraft.

The equipment is totally passive until activated by an enemy locked-on or tracking radar. It then acts automatically. For this reason MATILDA provides the Command with positive operational advantages. Being passive and automatic it continues to carry out its protective role when radar silence is imposed on the vessel, and irrespective of the state of fatigue of the crew. It does not require an operator to monitor the display unit nor does it react to irrelevant extraneous information. It attracts the attention of the Command only when a threat is positively detected from either missile or fire control radars.

TECHNIQUES STIMULATED BY ESM

The development of ESM equipment has stimulated a range of special techniques which are of technical interest in themselves. The design philosophy upon which equipment is based required many components including the travelling wave tube and in the more recent years solid state microwave amplifiers, detectors and aerials which gave a uniformity of response over very wide frequency bands of typically an octave and more. New DF methods suitable for wide band operation were devised including the switching and storage technique which combined simultaneous amplitude comparison with the sequential switching of one receiver around an array of fixed aerials. The instantaneous frequency measurement method for centrimetric waves was evolved with great success. New forms of display were developed in which an intercept was shown as a radial line indicating the bearing or as a point in a two-dimensional plot indicating frequency and bearing.

Much new knowledge was obtained on modes of electromagnetic propagation by scatter and duct effects. Rapid data handling for signal analysis was developed into practically effective methods for shipboard use. Altogether a new range of techniques has been evolved which in turn enrich electronic technology generally and find application elsewhere. The keynote of EW design philosophy is that of broad band, non-scanning, 100 per cent intercept probability systems and this has persisted to give a distinctive characteristic to ESM equipment.

4

Active Electronic Warfare—ECM

THE ROLE OF ECM

Electronic countermeasures attempt to achieve two main objectives by the use of a large and varied array of quite different devices. One is to disrupt surveillance and communication so that an enemy is unable to make the best, or sometimes even any, use of his electronic information gathering sensors such as surveillance radar or from the radio communication equipment which serve his command and control requirements. The other objective is to reduce the lethality of his weapons, guns and missiles, which depend on electronics for aiming, guidance or homing, by making some or all of his shots miss their targets. There are many ways in which these two objectives are pursued in the practice of ECM and a number of them will be discussed below. Frequently there are complications such as the effect of ECM on own ship's weapons. These can involve considerable complexity in the precautions taken in using ECM but this aspect will not be described.

RADAR NOISE JAMMING

A transmission at the frequency of a radar modulated by noise has the well known effect of saturating the radar receiver and causing its display to be covered by a continuous noisy paint which obscures targets the radar would otherwise see. Certainly a surveillance radar is disrupted and confused in its operation by this action, but its loss is not total as the jamming at least establishes the presence of a hostile warship. More seriously, the jamming signal can act as a homing beacon for missiles, and most missiles have a home-on-jam capability.

Against gunnery radars, in cases where shells have no homing ability, the effect of the noise jammer is to deny range information to the radar which seriously reduces or destroys, the lethality of the gun. However, naval gunfire is not a serious threat to ships in modern times. Missiles are, and the use of a noise jammer can be counter-productive since missiles do not need accurate ranging but they do need to select a warship target.

Thus, on balance the noise jammer, which was really the first ECM device to be conceived, is too dangerous for ships and has been largely replaced by other more effective and more subtle devices. The noise jammer in its original simple form is actually rather a blunt instrument which can rebound on the user. Its prime contribution in denying range information to a radar is not an important requirement and its role in naval warfare is now not very significant. However, modern forms of noise jamming using pulses of noise in conjunction with false target generators play a useful role in causing confusion, and this type of jammer is discussed below.

INFRA-RED JAMMING

Infra-red jammers help helicopters, and possibly small naval craft also, when threatened by heat-seeking missiles fired from shoulder launchers or ground installations. Devices of this type are generally simple to install and automatic in operation; they do not need a separate missile approach warner and the pilot can leave them alone after switching on. Generally, omni-directional coverage in azimuth is provided and the equipments are simple, robust and easy to monitor and maintain. Such an equipment is provided by British Aerospace where it is believed that the most effective means of providing protection for helicopters against infra-red homing missiles is to fit an active infra-red jamming device. This emits modulated IR energy, which when received in the missile homing head renders the guidance system ineffective. Such a system provides continuous protection throughout the mission.

The jammer is intended to be mounted externally on the helicopter, and operates by radiating modulated energy from an IR source. The output from the jammer is modulated mechanically by means of shutters. This output signal enters the missile seeker head, impairing its ability to track the target.

The IR source is a graphite radiating element, which is hermetically sealed within a sapphire envelope. The optical assembly which surrounds the lamp, rotating at high speed, passes between the lamp and slots in the outer drum. The drive to the optical assembly comes directly from a brushless DC motor integrally contained within the jammer mounting structure. Surrounding the optical system is a cylinder with 16 longitudinal slots spaced around its circumference. The slots are covered by a window, which provides environmental protection to the working parts, and also serves to transmit IR wavelength radiation, and to block visible emissions. The jammer is therefore covert in the visible region.

The modulated IR signal emitted by the jammer has the effect of degrading the tracking ability of IR homing missiles beyond the point at which they can be effective. The jammer radiates adequate power in the spectral band used by the seeker head of these missiles to protect most helicopter types.

Fields of view of 360 degrees in azimuth and ± 30 degrees in elevation can be provided. These fields of view apply to the jammer prior to installation on a helicopter, which may cause some blind arcs in practice.

It requires less than 2 kilowatts of primary power, its weight is 18 kilogrammes and it represents a useful operational capability which can be provided by electronic warfare particularly to helicopters, which tend to be vulnerable to attack from small infra-red homing missiles. The device is illustrated in Figure 4.1.

COMMUNICATIONS JAMMING

Communications jamming with a noise-modulated signal is quite different in its significance and potential. The message content of the enemy signal can be totally obscured and a definite advantage gained without incurring any potential risk to the jamming ship or shore base in the simplest cases. However, if a communication signal is jammed it cannot usually be read by the jamming ship. It could be tactically more valuable to read an enemy's signals than to stop him reading them, so this must be considered within the framework of command and control. If the enemy signal is encrypted, so that it cannot be read quickly or easily, then jamming can be more profitable and all that is given away is the presence of a jamming warship. To avoid

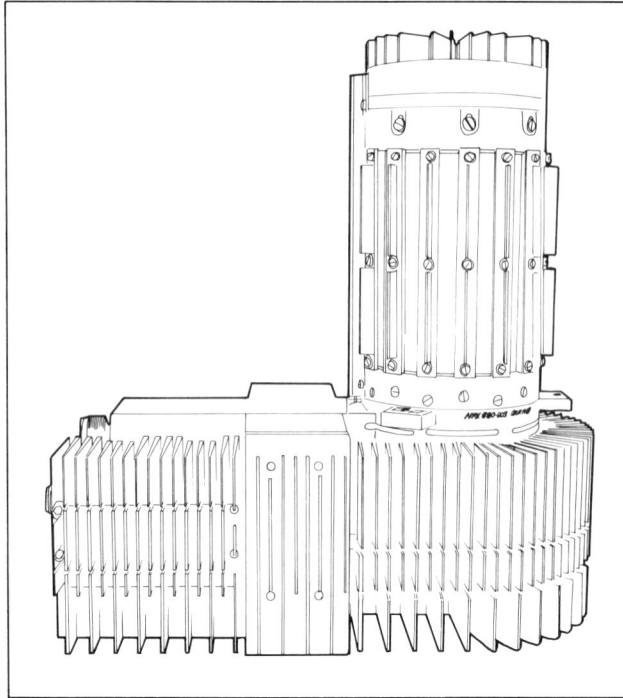

FIG. 4.1   An Infra-red Jammer *(British Aerospace)*

jamming, the enemy transmission could employ 'agility'—that is frequency hopping over quite a wide band. To jam this form of signal either an agile jammer or a broad band jammer would be required. This introduces undesirable features of considerable extra cost in the jammer and means that it may interfere with communications on its own ship. So a decision based on the balance of advantage must be made, as in most applications of EW. The stage has now been reached that while communications jamming can be very effective it is no longer a simple and inexpensive operation against modern frequency agile communications systems.

ELECTRONIC FALSE TARGETS

It can be dangerous to employ simple, continuous noise jamming against a surveillance radar, with the main attendant risk of providing a home-on-jam capability for missiles. It is possible to confuse the radar operator, who is trying to select a target for his missile, with a great number of false targets around the ship. These targets can be generated electronically and injected into the radar through its sidelobes as well as its main lobe. The appearance of these false targets on the radar display can be very realistic and the operator is certain to be confused to some extent. But he knows a warship target is there, somewhere, in the midst of all the painted targets and he can fire a missile.

Then the radar in the eye of the missile will look for a target to lock on to, and it will search the area in front of it. If the ship is within the search area of the missile, it is most likely to be selected because the missile cannot lock onto an electronic false target. This is because they have no physical reality in space and they will disappear when the missile radar stops scanning and attempts to lock on. So while the surveillance radar may be confused, there is not much prospect of a reduction in lethality of the missile. These sophisticated and elegant electronic false target generators are quite expensive and unfortunately their real application is limited to confusion in radar surveillance. This may allow the ship more time to take defensive action and deploy decoys. Of course if the missile uses infra-red homing the electronic false targets do not affect it at all.

Thus, in theory, the electronic false target generator alone is not always of prime naval significance because it has only a limited potential for reducing missile lethality, this being the prime requirement of the ship being attacked. Nevertheless, in practice, false target generators have proved to be an embarrassment to attackers launching missiles against ships and it seems that their tactical value is, currently, quite considerable. Commercial equipments combine false target generation with other jamming modes and collectively these are effective in reducing the lethality of attacks.

BREAK-LOCK DEVICES

If a missile has locked on to a ship it is possible, by electronic means, to break the lock in range and also, with some types of missile homing, to break the lock in angle as well. This is achieved by creating electronically, in the missile's radar, a strong false target greater than that of the ship and 'capturing' the lock. The false target is moved away in range or angle with the missile following, and then switched off. The missile is left without a target and is forced to search again. If there is a strong decoy target placed nearby, the missile has a high probability of locking on to this, provided it is a real physical object in space. This combination of a break-lock device and decoys is effective in reducing lethality when a ship has actually been selected as a target and a missile is homing to it.

It is rather more difficult to break lock in angle than in range, especially if the missile is using a simultaneous lobing method of guidance for homing. If sequential-lobing, such as the well-known conical scanning technique, is used a missile can be pulled off in angle. This is not so good as range break lock since the angle pull-off may result only in the missile reaching its target by a curved rather than a straight line.

TYPES OF JAMMER

One effective commercial equipment provides electronic false targets and a capability for pulling off a missile in range and angle. It is known as GUARDIAN and is a product of Thorn EMI.

GUARDIAN is a sophisticated self-contained electronic counter measures system in production for naval use. It is a fully responsive system providing area and point defence against surveillance, target indication and missile homing radars and has the capability to counter Multiple Simultaneous Threats.

Modular construction is utilised and the system is suitable for installation in aircraft carriers, destroyers and frigates. It can also be installed in a transportable shelter, and as a self contained unit, can be deployed on floating or land bases.

In area defence, when protection is provided for a task force, convoy or a single unit, pulse and/or noise signal patterns are generated to counter and confuse surveillance, target indication, and (before lock-on) missile homing radars. In point defence, signals are generated to counter missile homing systems, and after lock-on, to produce Range Gate and Angle pull-offs.

The GUARDIAN system utilises two steerable antenna assemblies to ensure an uninterrupted 360 degree coverage, with elevation cover up to 50 degrees. The assemblies can be installed port and starboard or alternatively fore and aft and each is auto-stabilised for pitch and roll.

Control of the overall system is from a 'user friendly' console which incorporates a clear display. Structured modular software is utilised for a fast real time response, with software controlled system management and interfacing for integration with the ship's other systems if required.

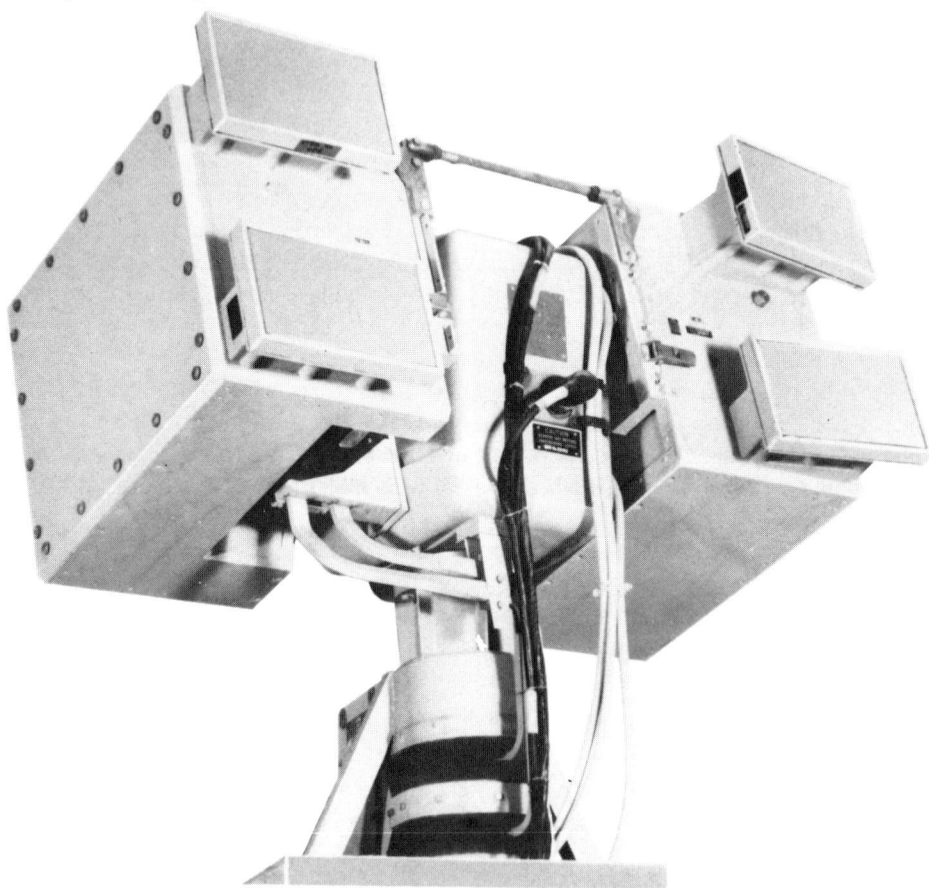

FIG. 4.2   GUARDIAN ECM Aerials (Thorn EMI)

Received signals from direction finding antennas on each antenna assembly are analysed for threat evaluation utilising a comprehensive electronic library and the appropriate countermeasures are automatically selected. The high power transmitting systems have the capability of jamming operations against several types of target simultaneously. Modular software and hardware design enables an extension of operating capability if so required.

The GUARDIAN antenna assembly is shown in Figure 4.2 and its operator console in Figure 4.3.

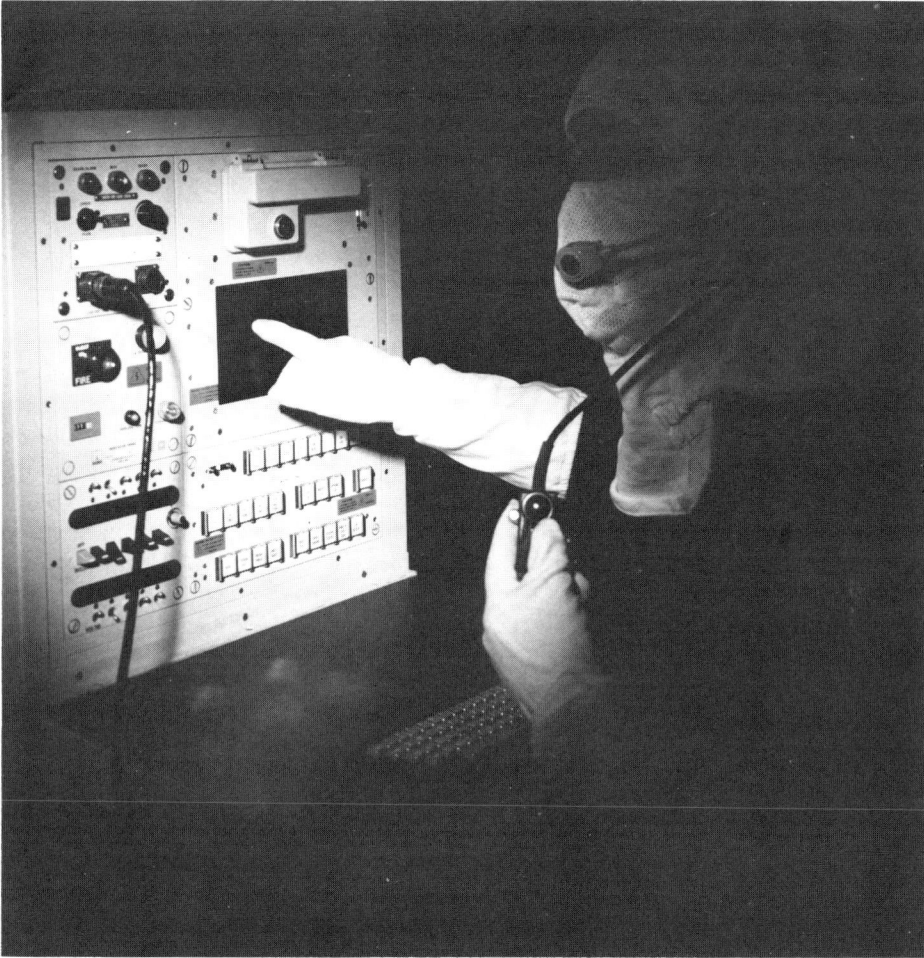

FIG. 4.3   GUARDIAN ECM Operator's Console *(Thorn EMI)*

ACTIVE JAMMERS

Active jammers may be used for area defence or point defence.

Area defence jammers are sophisticated systems, which may be installed in selected ships to give protection to a task group. They can act as 'Force Multipliers' by injecting false targets into the side lobes of hostile surveillance radars. These false targets can be made to give false target tracks, which are independent of the jammers own platform movement. Point defence jammers are conversely designed to give protection to a single unit. Although these jammers can generate false targets, such targets will move in unison with the jammer platform. SCIMITAR, provided by the MEL company, is typical of modern point defence jammers.

The prime threat to surface ships is the anti-ship missile launched at varying ranges and heights from surface craft, submarines, aircraft and helicopters. Recent conflicts have demonstrated the devastating destructive effect of short-range subsonic, sea-skimming missiles launched from aircraft or a shore-based site. The next generation pose a much greater threat. Some types, already in service, can be launched from greater distances, travel at speeds in the order of Mach 2.5 and arrive on target from elevations varying between sea-level and high dive angles.

Irrespective of launch platform however, most attacks follow a three stage sequence, namely:

> Detection and designation of target by enemy search radars
> Missile launch and initial flight pattern using a pre-programmed flight path, or transmitted guidance information
> Terminal homing for the final phase using a radar located in the missile head

SCIMITAR counters all stages of any missile attack using a variety of electronic noise and deception techniques, either singly or in combination, to make target designation and target lock-on impossible. If missile lock-on has already occurred, SCIMITAR will cause the missile to lose track of its designated target. By jamming enemy radars, SCIMITAR also reduces the effectiveness of enemy aircraft and gunfire.

This sophisticated jammer consists of two identical antenna systems, which are mounted on either side of a mast structure. These are fed with RF energy from the main RF cabinet, placed at or near to the bottom of the mast. The jamming response is automatically controlled by the processing cabinet. There is a local control box but this is only used in an emergency, when all other modes of control have failed. Under normal modes of operation, the jammer would either be controlled from the Tactical Data Handling Systems or directly from an ESM system. In this mode of control, the jammer is fed with a target bearing and a designated radar to jam, as determined by the ESM system. The jammer then assigns an antenna system to the threat and slews the appropriate antenna to the required bearing. At the same time the target characteristics are derived from the jammers own 'look-up library' and the system then goes into the search mode. Each antenna system consists of an upper receiving antenna and a lower transmitting antenna. In the search mode the receive antenna searches about the designated bearing until it locates a target, which matches the designated library information.

When the required target has been acquired, the system will lock onto and track the target. When this has been achieved, the jammer will start a pre-programmed response as determined by the function generators housed in the processing cabinet. In the RF cabinet there are two travelling wave tubes, one providing a continuous wave (CW) response and the other a pulsed response. The tubes are continuously tunable over the range 7.5–16.5 GHz. SCIMITAR is what is known as a responsive jammer. This means that if, for example, it is required to jam a pulsed radar, the receiver system will look for the required pulse and as soon as this is received an exactly similar pulse will be generated by the RF system. This jamming pulse will then be seen as a false echo by the enemy radar. The pulsed response can be used in conjunction with a noise signal from the CW TWT or noise only jamming can be transmitted. In addition to these general modes, special techniques can be used against tracking radars, such as spin frequency modulation (SFM) or range gate pull off (RGPO). If a tracking radar is using conical scan then SFM will give the tracking radar a false bearing or elevation signal. In the case of a sea skimming missile, this could divert the missile away from the target. In the case of a monopulse radar, then provided the system response is rapid enough, the jamming pulse can be inserted as a false echo, into the range gate of the tracking radar. Once inserted the false echo can be driven away in time from the true echo. Once again considering a sea skimming missile this will cause the missile to lose lock, on the target ship. In summary Scimitar provides the following jamming response:

CW Noise
Pulse Noise
Scan Rate Modulation (SRM)
Inverted Scan Rate Modulation (ISRM)
Swept Scan Rate Modulation (SSRM)
Range Gate Pull Off (RGPO).

These jamming modes can be applied separately or in various combinations.

Because of its dual antenna configuration, SCIMITAR can engage separate targets on either side of the ship or two targets in the same beam. Also, because the processing cabinet contains two function generators, whilst one target is being jammed, a sequence for the next most threatening target may be set up and applied immediately the first target has been successfully jammed.

SCIMITAR is a powerful and sophisticated ECM system which jams all phases of an attack, including surveillance, target indication, acquisition and terminal homing.

It covers 360 degrees in azimuth and 0–70 degrees in elevation. Separate groups of targets can be tracked and jammed by each of the two antennas, thus enabling the system to counter a wide variety of threats simultaneously. This is essential in a multi-threat situation when the ship is under attack from enemy ships and missiles. SCIMITAR can be integrated with any modern Electronic Support Measures system. Its normal mode of operation is automatic with target assignment being controlled from the ESM console or the Ship's Tactical Data-handling System. In the event of damage to the ESM System, SCIMITAR can be operated manually as a stand-alone defence measure which could be crucial in the event of damage to the ESM System.

In essence the types of operational advantage claimed for SCIMITAR may be summarized along the following lines.

(i) In a multi-threat situation SCIMITAR can operate to provide protective screening to a fleet. This action is characterized by a block of noise 4 kilometres wide by 8 kilometres deep. Most in-service point defence systems cannot cope with a saturation attack by multiple targets. It is essential therefore to neutralise the effectiveness of the launch platforms and to decoy as many missiles as possible so as to eliminate or minimize the hard kill requirement. SCIMITAR engages a number of targets simultaneously at long range and when success has been achieved, automatically switches to the next priority threat. Often the first indication of probable hostility is when ESM systems indicate that an enemy target indication or tracking radar is locked-on. An immediate response is required to delay the onset of hostilities and to gain time for tactical deployment and SCIMITAR provides that response by jamming or confusing enemy radars, denying them the ability to launch a missile attack.

(ii) By radiating in a number of different modes SCIMITAR makes it very difficult for an enemy operator to detect and designate target ships.

(iii) An anti-ship missile travelling at high speed presents a very small radar signature and is virtually undetectable by most surveillance radars currently at sea and area defence missile systems designated to operate at 50–100 kilometres are thus rendered ineffective. However, incoming missiles are detected by modern ESM systems and by working automatically with such ESM systems, SCIMITAR rapidly analyses the radar threat and counters it electronically while it is still at long range.

COMPREHENSIVE ECM FOR MAJOR WARSHIPS

A multiple jamming equipment for major warships is provided by Racal and is known as CYGNUS. It gives a number of ECM modes and is typical of the type of comprehensive ECM equipments now available for the navies of the world.

The CYGNUS system is designed to integrate with any ESM system capable of providing approximate frequency and bearing data and is particularly compatible with the Racal CUTLASS family. This integration will provide an automatic electronic countermeasure system suitable for one man operation. The system is also capable of an autonomous ECM function when not coupled to any form of ESM equipment.

The CYGNUS jammer operates over the 8–16 GHz frequency range and provides a radar jamming capability resulting in a high degree of protection against radar associated threats.

The system can provide both responsive noise and deception jamming for use in the following roles:

> To jam early warning radars and target acquisition radars, whether surface, airborne or ground based.
> To unlock missile guidance radars on launch platforms.
> To jam missile guidance radars on active homing missiles.

It gives an automatic jamming response to threat emitters and transmits a narrow pencil beam which is automatically kept locked onto the threat, using a tracking receiver. This technique enables a very high Effective Radiated Power (ERP)—of the order of 300 kilowatts—to be achieved, which produces a long range performance and short distance burn-through capability. When coupled to an ESM System, signal parameters of the emitter selected for jamming are passed automatically to the ECM processor. These parameters will normally include frequency, bearing and time of arrival (TOA) information. The tracking receiver then locks onto and tracks the signal in azimuth, elevation and Radio Frequency (RF). RF at the tracking frequency is then modulated, using a selected modulation response, amplified and transmitted as a jamming signal. An operator control may be set to instruct the jammer automatically to acquire the signal and jam with the most efficient response, or it may be manually programmed to transmit an operator-selected response. When used with a CUTLASS ESM system the most effective response against an emitter is automatically obtained from the library.

The ability of CYGNUS accurately to track a target in both azimuth and elevation allows for effective jamming of airborne targets.

The bearing obtained by the system is accurate to 1 degree rms and is available for use by other weapons systems for such applications as target acquisition or weapon aiming. The need for active transmission from the installation's own radars is therefore eliminated, reducing the possibility of detection from enemy ESM systems.

The aerial and control panel are shown in Figure 4.4.

FIG. 4.4   The CYGNUS Aerial and Control Panel.
A Jammed Radar Display and the Transmitted
Jammer Spectrum *(Racal Radar Defence Systems)*

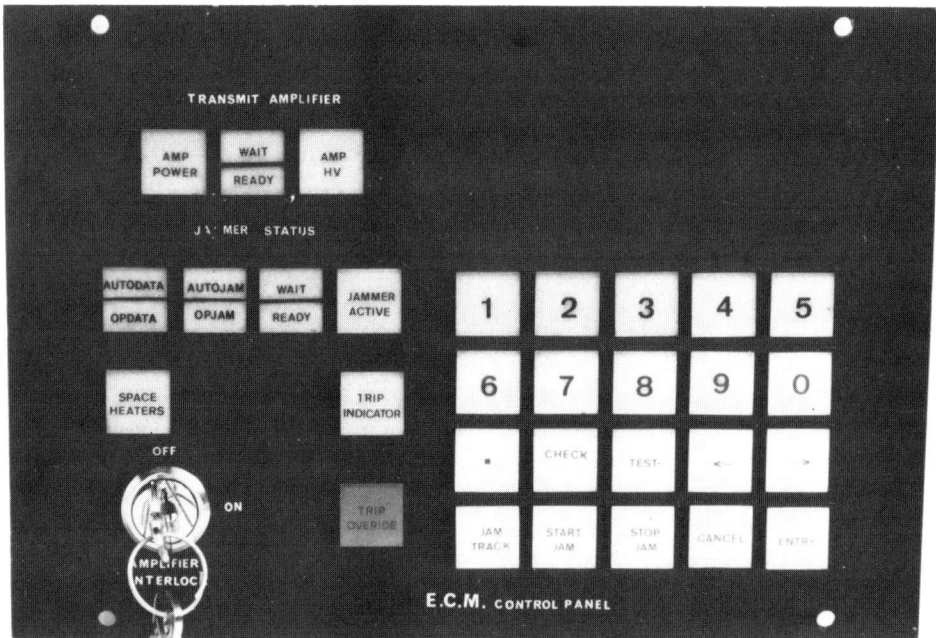

The system carries out four major tasks on receipt of initial jamming information:

Approximate frequency and bearing of the emitter, obtained from either the ESM system or manually entered by the operator, are used to initially set-on tracking receiver frequency and jammer antenna bearing respectively.

The tracking receiver acquires and tracks the emitter accurately in azimuth and elevation. This brings the jamming antenna into accurate alignment with the threat.

The frequency of the threat emitter is locked onto and tracked to within 1MHz.

RF at the lock-on frequency is modulated by the Modulator/Transmitter Interface Unit, using the selected modulation response, amplified by the High Power Amplifier and then transmitted. Transmission takes the form of a narrow, less than 5 degrees beamwidth, high Effective Radiated Power signal emitted from the jamming dish antenna.

When the system receives a threat emitting a continuous wave signal, bearing information may not be available to the processor and in this case a search mode is initiated to find the signal.

The operation of the ECM system is controlled from the ECM Control Panel. This is normally contained within the ESM Console which is then operated by a single EW operator.

Several types of modulation are available to suit the nature of the threat including:

Track-while-scan
Monopulse
Fixed Conscan (Auto)
Fixed Conscan (Manual)
Swept Conscan
False Target
Swept Spot
Noise Spot
Amplitude Modulation
Rangegate Pull Off (RGPO)
Continuous Wave (CW)

Some of these are discussed below:

Track-While-Scan is used against scanning radars which are identified by the detection of groups of pulses (scan burst) occurring at regular intervals as the enemy scanning antenna rotates. The jamming response generated takes the form of a burst of noise which, because of its effect on the enemy AGC at the ranges this response is normally used, produces what is termed 'black hole jamming'.

The burst of noise (noise bandwidth = 10 MHz), is produced 120 microseconds after the fourth pulse received by the tracking receiver and lasts for 100 ms. The first four pulses are allowed through to enable tracking to take place. Since these pulses are received at the edge of the enemy beam as it scans across the jamming platform, the signal to noise ratio is at its worst. The effects are:

Demands on the tracking receiver sensitivity are high, but the second two pulses received ensures accurate tracking.

Echoes from the jamming location as a result of these four pulses are unlikely to be detected by the enemy radar.

The delay of 120 microseconds ensures that the jamming does not appear on the enemy Plan Position Indicator at a position coincident with the position of the jamming platform. If the jamming platform is within ten miles of the outer edge of the enemy radar display, the jamming, which would normally appear before any AGC action occurs, will be out of range.

The 100 millisecond period of jamming is normally sufficient to jam the remainder of the scan burst. If not, a second burst is produced. At the end of the jamming period the jammer remains blanked until the next scan burst is detected.

Monopulse Response is used against lock-on radars and there must be the minimum delay between receipt of an enemy emitter pulse and transmission of the jamming signals.

25 microsecond pulses of noise modulated RF (Noise Bandwidth 1–20 MHz) are transmitted after each received pulse. This continues for 5 seconds and is followed by 5 seconds of silence before jamming continues.

Fixed Conscan is for use against conical scanning lock-on radars. The characteristics of the echoes received by the enemy lock-on radar are:

> When not on target, the amplitude of the echoes varies sinusoidally at the conscan (nutation) frequency. The phase of the conscan envelope informs the lock-on radar in which direction it is off target.
>
> The difference in the amplitude of the echoes reduces as the radar approaches 'lock-on' so that, when on target the amplitude of the echoes are constant throughout 360 degrees of the aerial nutation.

The purpose of conscan jamming is to modulate the RF carrier with square wave gated noise (noise bandwidth 1–20 MHz) at a gating frequency which is, in the following order of preference:

> Exactly equal to the conscan frequency of the threat radar.
> As close as possible to the conscan frequency of the threat radar.
> Being slowly swept through the conscan frequency of the threat radar.

The aim of this is to superimpose amplitude variations on the echoes received by the threat radar and cause it to unlock.

Tracking takes place in each non-transmitting half cycle of the gated noise. The active periods of gated noise last for approximately 5 seconds and alternate with quiescent periods also of 5 seconds approximate duration.

In the fixed conscan (Auto) mode, the gating frequency (between 10Hz and 300 Hz) is automatically set at the value of the conscan frequency as measured by the ESM system and is automatically transferred from the ESM processor without operator intervention.

In *False Target Jamming* the purpose is to present a number of false targets to an enemy surveillance or navigational radar which appear to be moving relative to the real target. The production of these false targets is triggered by pulses arriving from the threat radar and they are therefore synchronous with the radar PRF.

Time delays are introduced between the received pulse and the false target pulses so that the false targets always appear, on the enemy display, at a greater range than the real target. The time delays are controlled by the ECM system software and the false target pulses are generated under control of this software.

At the onset of jamming, each false target pulse is produced at a different initial delay. Each of these delays is progressively increased or decreased by the software so that, over a period of time, the targets appear on the enemy display to be moving relative to the real target. This movement results from the vectorial addition of:

> The speed and direction of the jamming ship.
>
> The software generated speed and direction of the false targets with respect to the real target. The software generated direction will be either towards or away from the real target (delay decrease or increase respectively).

Three false targets are produced each time the enemy radar beam sweeps across the ECM location.

Spot Jamming is the transmission of an RF carrier which is modulated by continuous random noise. There are three noise bandwidth ranges:

> Variable between 1 MHz and 20 MHz
>
> 40 MHz
>
> 200 MHz

In all cases, there is a short period for look through, after 128 ms of jamming, to allow continued tracking to take place. The first two pulses at the beginning of every active period are allowed through for frequency and angle tracking purposes. Jamming is delayed a further 120 microseconds on the second pulse so that the start of jamming does not appear coincident with the position of the jamming ship.

Jamming may either be continuous or 'blinked'. 'Blinked' mode modulation provides alternating 5 seconds active and quiescent periods.

Swept spot is similar to Noise Spot except that there is no 'look through' and the frequency of the RF carrier is swept. No tracking is therefore able to take place. The operator selects the range of sweep within the limits of ± 500 MHz of the carrier frequency and the software automatically varies the sweep rate randomly between 0 Hz and 100 Hz.

In *Amplitude Modulation Jamming,* the operator can select a modulation frequency in the range 0.5 MHz to 10 MHz for square wave amplitude modulation.

In the *Range Gate Pull Off* (RGPO) mode, the initial deception pulse of the RGPO sequence is transmitted as soon after the received pulse as possible and the delay time of this jamming pulse from receipt of the radar pulse does not exceed 200 nanoseconds. The deception pulse is progressively delayed to seduce the threat emitter away from the real target by creating a false target. Seduction range is determined by the acceleration, maximum velocity and duration of the transmitted response. These parameters are pre-programmable so that the false target appears to move realistically to its new position, thus controlling the range gate.

Jamming ceases after the transmit time and the radar, having lost the target inside its range gate, is forced into a search mode. It would now be quite likely to re-acquire the ship and continue guiding the weapon. However, if decoys are deployed early in the RGPO jamming sequence, the radar is provided with a target on which to lock. In case this does not happen, the jammer remains quiescent for the silent time and then repeats the process and continues repeating it automatically.

DECOYS

Decoys, real rather than false electronic targets, are by far the most potent form of ECM in providing protection to ships through reducing the lethality of missiles. If a ship receives warning, including target identity, from its ESM equipment that a missile attack is imminent, its course of action is to lay down a pattern of decoys around itself. The attacking aircraft then sees a number of radar contacts in a group; these are all 'real' targets in that they provide a radar echo from a point in space and they are capable of being locked onto. If the aircraft selects any of the decoys for its missiles, and the missiles home to these, then dilution of the attack occurs because some or all of the missiles are wasted.

If a missile is approaching the real ship and would acquire it, but is seeing also close to the ship a bigger decoy target, it will select the bigger target and is thereby distracted. If the real ship is actually selected by the missile (which the ship may know from the pattern of behaviour of the intercepted missile signal) it can deploy a decoy above or beside itself which the missile will see as part of the ship echo. The ship then moves away from the decoy and the missile stays locked to the bigger decoy; this is known as seduction. In all of these cases, the attack lethality can be substantially reduced and the chance of the ship's survival increased in a very cost-effective manner.

Deployment of Decoys

Distraction decoys are presented as alternative targets to a missile radar during its search phase. To be effective, the decoy must be deployed at a range and position such that it is encountered and 'locked on' to by the missile radar before it sees the target ship. For the decoy to be accepted it must have characteristics sufficiently resembling the radar signature of an intended target.

In practice this means that the radar cross-section of the decoy at the time of missile search need only exceed the 'threshold' level equivalent to a minimum intended target signature, and not necessarily be identical to the particular target signature presented in the absence of a decoy. Where the missile mode of search may be unknown to the defending ship, Distraction decoys may be launched in patterns about the ship in such a way that a decoy will be encountered first and accepted by a missile with any search mode or incoming bearing. The range of deployment and positioning should be such that the decoys are neither too distant to fall within the search area nor too close to enable an initially distracted missile to locate the ship and manoeuvre toward it should the character of the decoy become apparent.

In order to achieve the most cost effective use of Distraction decoys, it is necessary to provide the maximum practical duration of cover. This is particularly necessary when the ship must be defended against multiple threats of uncertain timing. Prolonged protection can be achieved by matching initial positioning to the prevalent wind conditions, and by manoeuvring the ship to maintain its relative position within the decoy pattern. Alternatively the ship may proceed on course, progressively replacing as necessary those decoys which no longer remain within acceptable range.

Such tactical requirements necessitate an automatically variable decoy range so that fuze setting for decoy deployment may need to be varied between typically about 3 and 16 seconds according to relative wind strength and direction in the case of airborne decoys.

When decoy deployment is by means of rockets fired from the ship the launcher elevation and azimuth angles although fixed, are selected to suit the rocket performance and enable a basic pattern of usually four decoys to be so placed in height and range that good duration of protection can be achieved despite considerable ship roll and pitch. The launch system capabilities normally include such facilities for decoy deployment.

The decoy system operation providing good Distraction mode requirements are usually:

Minimum Pattern Deployment Time
This is achieved by pre-selection of required firing directions so that only a single firing operation can deploy the pattern.

Minimum Manual Intervention
This is normally achieved by automatic fuze time selection to suit the pre-selected bearings. Ultimate manual firing is usually retained since Distraction mode decoy deployment can frequently be a precautionary measure inappropriate for automatic triggering by a threat warning system.

Wind Effect Corrections
Decoy systems normally take account of relative wind speed and direction such that the deployment range is automatically selected to prolong the decoy effective life.

Decoy Replacement Warning
Where wind data is taken into account by the system, the critical decoy of the initial pattern can be determined and its predicted duration of effectiveness displayed as a warning of the time at which decoy replacement will be necessary.

Discretion on whether to deploy at this time remains with the system operator who may be guided by direct decoy position monitoring and an assessment of whether continued protection is necessary.

Fallback Operational Modes
Although automatic selection may be provided, manual selection is also usually available as a fallback in the event of non-availability of wind data. Local control in the vicinity of each launcher location enables distraction decoys to be launched independently of the system command module.

Seduction decoys are deployed with the aim of breaking the 'lock' of a missile which has already located the target ship, so that a course deflection occurs and a direct hit is avoided. Seduction decoys can be used to extend the target in such a way that the apparent 'centroid' of the combined ship and decoy radar cross-section distribution is moved progressively away from that part of the ship on which the missile would otherwise impact.

For the 'Centroid' decoy to be effective, it must be deployed rapidly to reach a radar cross-section of comparable order to that of the target ship, and have such characteristics that it is effective in moving the aiming point of the missile away from the ship. Since a missile homing by active radar can be considered to have located its target within range and azimuth limits, it is essential that Seduction decoys reach an effective radar cross-section within the cell so defined, i.e. within the missile's range gate.

The size of the cell within which co-location of ship and decoy is initially necessary depends upon the characteristics of the missile radar and the missile range. Practical co-location depends upon the time the decoy takes to reach effective decoy dimensions, and the wind speed and direction relative to the target ship. The decoy is positioned accordingly.

The system requirement for Seduction Decoy protection is therefore that the above conditions be effectively met in the minimum practicable reaction time. The operational advantages to be gained are considerable. A large radar cross-section may be achieved by effectively creating a decoy at short range and a height such that the radar cross-section can be enhanced by multipath reflection from the sea surface. The launch system should deploy multiple munitions on the same or adjacent bearings when necessary to maximize the decoy radar cross-section.

Since minimum reaction time is a key requirement, fully automatic deployment is usually provided where suitable data inputs can be arranged. In an automatic mode of control the decoy system selects and directs the optimum deployment of the Seduction Decoy such that wind and threat information are used to optimize salvo type, size, range, bearing, firing time, and firing interval.

A desirable operational concept for Seduction protection is that the decoy system should be integrated with the ship's EW system, and because of the number of variables affecting the degree of protection, that the potential for human delay or error be eliminated wherever practical by the use of a simple data processor.

Naval vessels emit Infra-Red radiation across a broad spectrum which contrasts with the natural background emissions of the sea and sky. The transmission of infra-red energy is affected by the absorption of carbon dioxide and water vapour molecules in specific bands in the IR spectrum. There are however two 'windows' where attenuation is minimal and where a typical ship produces relatively large amounts of radiated energy. These are in the 3 to 5 micron band and the 8 to 14 micron band. The shorter wavelength contains energy which is generated principally by the 'Hot Spots' of the ship such as engine exhausts, whereas the longer wavelength is produced primarily by the 'cool' ship's hull and superstructure.

An attacking missile equipped with an IR seeker can make use of this radiation signature to find its target and to discriminate between a real ship and a simple decoy.

A simple decoy is defined as one which produces effective radiation in one band only—usually 3–5 micron or 'hot spot'.

Positioning of an IR decoy relative to the target ship is of critical importance. If the attacking missile has acquired the target ship with its IR seeker, the decoy, if it is to be effective must be deployed in the Centroid mode of defence, i.e. the decoy and target ship must both be seen within the IR seeker beam width so that the combined effect is to bias the seeker towards the Centroid between ship and decoy. It is always desirable to bias the attack toward the decoy radiation cell by presenting the decoy as a powerful preferential target.

It is often possible to use the relative wind vector to cause the decoy and ship to separate during the terminal IR engagement. There can, however, be tactical situations where the relative wind can approach zero. In these circumstances, it is desirable that the decoy can be deployed in such a way that there is an apparent ship and decoy separation. This is achieved by multiple reseeding of IR decoys at progressively increasing range to create a radiating target that appears to move away from the ship.

A further constraint is imposed upon the IR decoy position: that of height above the sea. If the missile attack is based on sea skimming tactics, the look-up angle of the seeker will be kept to the lowest value consistent with the target acquisition. Ideally perhaps an IR decoy should be placed not much more than 20 metres above the sea surface. However, the effectiveness is not seriously diminished if the decoy initiation height is set at a nominal 30 metres and followed by a slow descent towards the sea.

Deployment height above the sea is nominally 30 metres, so the deployment is tolerant to normal roll and pitch induced variations in launch elevation. The firing interval, payload fall rate and individual payload duration are such that up to four decoys may usually be effective simultaneously, giving a very large preferential target. However, the build up to the large radiation level is gradual with each successive mortaring until the high level is reached. By this means a sudden increase in overall ship/decoy target radiation intensity is avoided which could, in some circumstances, cause the seeker to reject the decoy.

Where, for example, combined Chaff and IR deployment is required, the decoy tactics should additionally provide the optimized IR deployment time and interval to give the best 'co-location' of the IR decoy with the calculated centroid locus produced by the combined ship and radar decoy in relation to the direction of the threat.

Groups of Target Selection Confusion decoys can be deployed at a manually pre-set range so that alternative targets are presented to hostile search and acquisition radars. The distribution of these decoys can be made to simulate the typical squadron separation of a group of missile boats by sequential firing to near maximum range combined with small alterations of course.

Where Distraction decoys have been deployed against an initial threat, the resulting pattern of decoys from the initial salvo and subsequent individual or pair replacements will present considerable difficulty to the hostile radars and afford a worthwhile degree of Confusion protection against subsequent attempted attack. An irregular pattern of decoys makes it particularly difficult to pick out the intended target. The duration of the decoys may be up to 15 minutes, thus allowing sufficient time for tactical manoeuvre.

'Dump' mode deployment of decoys can be controlled automatically in conjunction with a Range Gate Pull Off Jammer. In general the RGPO Jammer is used to move the missile lock a distance downthreat of the ship. The positioning of the decoy is made so that the Decoy return occurs in a credible position when the jammer is switched off.

The timing of the RGPO action and the co-ordination of the decoy deployment may be critical to the success of Dump mode protection. For best protection, the characteristics of jammer, decoys and deployment system require a dedicated software package taking into account variables such as pull-off rate, likely threat time to impact, wind speed and direction, and the decoy radar cross-section time characteristic.

Types of Decoy

Simple clouds of chaff and infra-red flares are used as decoys. They are effective against current radars and missile homing heads but it is now possible and it is claimed by sensor designers that new radar technology may be able to discriminate against chaff on the basis of the spectral characteristics of its echo. Nevertheless chaff is used widely today as a cost-effective radar decoy against current radars and it remains to be seen whether any future generation radars will be able to discriminate against it successfully.

New infra-red homing eyes will discriminate against simple flares on the basis of their temperature, which is too high to simulate a ship. More sophisticated decoys are now available using electronically generated radar decoying signals from equipment mounted in a container which is positioned in space by a rocket and suspended from a parachute. More sophisticated IR decoys are needed and some designs using low temperature, slow burning materials are probably representative of the next generation. Many other designs for decoys are being investigated. The essential features of low cost, rapid deployment, a reasonably long endurance and effectiveness against modern radar and IR homing heads in missiles present an engineering challenge of some substance to weapon designers. Nevertheless EW decoys are a most important and very effective element in a ship's defensive armoury.

Typical of present day chaff and IR decoys is the Plessey SHIELD system which comprises a set of launchers, control equipment and decoy munitions. The system provides both Distraction and Seduction (Centroid) protection for large or small Naval and Merchant ships. A comprehensive description of this system will illustrate the degree of engineering sophistication and complexity which modern EW decoys require to be effective at sea. They are, in fact, rather more complex than is generally appreciated.

Two versions of SHIELD are available, one having manually fuzed rockets for use with simple independent systems, the other having electronically fuzed rockets for use with the automatic system interfaced with the ship's own computer. The chaff decoy rockets and infra-red decoys give short range Seduction (Centroid) mode performance as well as Distraction mode capability.

A fixed-fin chaff rocket with plug and socket is also available. The system, which is designed for fast reaction, ease of installation, simplicity of operation and minimum maintenance, can be specified to suit ships of all sizes, and a limited initial installation can be economically upgraded should operational needs change or new payloads be introduced.

All-round protection is provided for corvettes or smaller vessels by two cross-barrel launchers, and for frigates and large vessels by four parallel launchers. Launchers are compact and transfer negligible loads to the deck, making structural reinforcement unnecessary. They make protection possible for ships of only a few hundred tons.

Inductive couplings permit easy loading and rounds need no maintenance throughout their life. Similar chaff munitions for all modes of operation greatly ease logistics problems. SHIELD rockets accelerate the chaff load to its location and deploy, typically, ninety-five per cent or more of the chaff effectively. Since each anti-ship missile exhibits a different characteristic, the SHIELD system is designed to provide flexibility in use and offers, from a single programmable round, seduction or distraction modes of operation and a decoy performance which can be predetermined by computer to match the threat environment.

SHIELD offers three modes of operation:

Distraction
Seduction Dump for association with: range gate stealing
Seduction Centroid to give centroidal shift in the point of lock of the missile

The selected mode of operation will depend upon the type of attack. By adjustment of the fuze release time the SHIELD system will give the required performance in each of these modes.

Distraction Decoy

This provides up to four separate decoy chaff clouds, deployed in a pattern surrounding the ship at a range of up to two kilometres depending on the fuze time selected. This mode of operation is particularly effective against simultaneous attacks from one or several directions. Under such an attack the majority of missiles will lock-on to decoys, leaving the ship to deal with the remaining threats by direct action, active ECM or other modes of operation.

At pre-determined intervals related to ship's speed, the foremost decoys are re-seeded to preserve the protection cover for the duration of the threat and, by individual fuze adjustment, decoys are biased into wind to prolong the cover.

Seduction Decoy—Dump

This mode is intended for use with active ECM range gate stealing equipment. It attracts the radar and transfers the missile range gate from the ship to a chaff cloud. The range of deployment for this is dependent upon the ECM and radar characteristics.

Seduction Decoy—Centroid

This mode of operation is automatic and is regarded as the last form of passive defence available. It requires the deployment of chaff close to the ship so that large chaff radar echoes remain as the ship moves on. The intention is to duplicate and amplify the radar echo of the ship. For large ships a number of chaff rockets are deployed to produce a suitable echo. The missile is decoyed sufficiently to avoid a direct hit. In this condition the system calculates and sets optimum fuze times, barrel selection, salvo size and time of fire.

When intelligence indicates that an unidentified threat might be a heat-seeker, SHIELD automatically deploys infra-red decoys and a progression of dual signature decoys shifts the IR centroid from the ship causing a steadily increasing diversion of the missile. Co-location or radar and IR Decoys is possible. If the signatures of a salvo of missiles include both radar homing and heat-seeking prints, SHIELD automatically deploys both types of decoy.

SHIELD is an integrated software-based decoy system. It features a memory compiled from extensive tactical engagement modelling, taking account of all likely threat scenarios. In operation, the system reacts automatically to a threat, calculates and sets optimum fuze times, barrel selection, salvo size and time of fire.

The control equipment includes a Command Module which is installed in the Command Control Centre and linked to the ship's sensors. The Command Module contains the tactical response of the SHIELD system and is the primary control unit for the system. It houses the central processor and tactics packages and has a front panel used for system selection options, manual data inputs and status displays. The Command Module acts as a data bus terminal so that microprocessors in the unit and in the Launcher Control Modules communicate data essentially by a twisted pair. The data bus system thus minimises inter-unit cabling requirements. The command Module also handles the interface with the ships data bus.

The front panel is used to select the required modes of control and deployment, and to display the loaded status of each launcher barrel. Operation is accessed by a key operated switch which turns on power and illuminates status. Initially the system will indicate that MANUAL control is selected, but alternative selector buttons offer options of AUTO, SEMI-AUTO, RELOAD or TEST/SET control functions. When

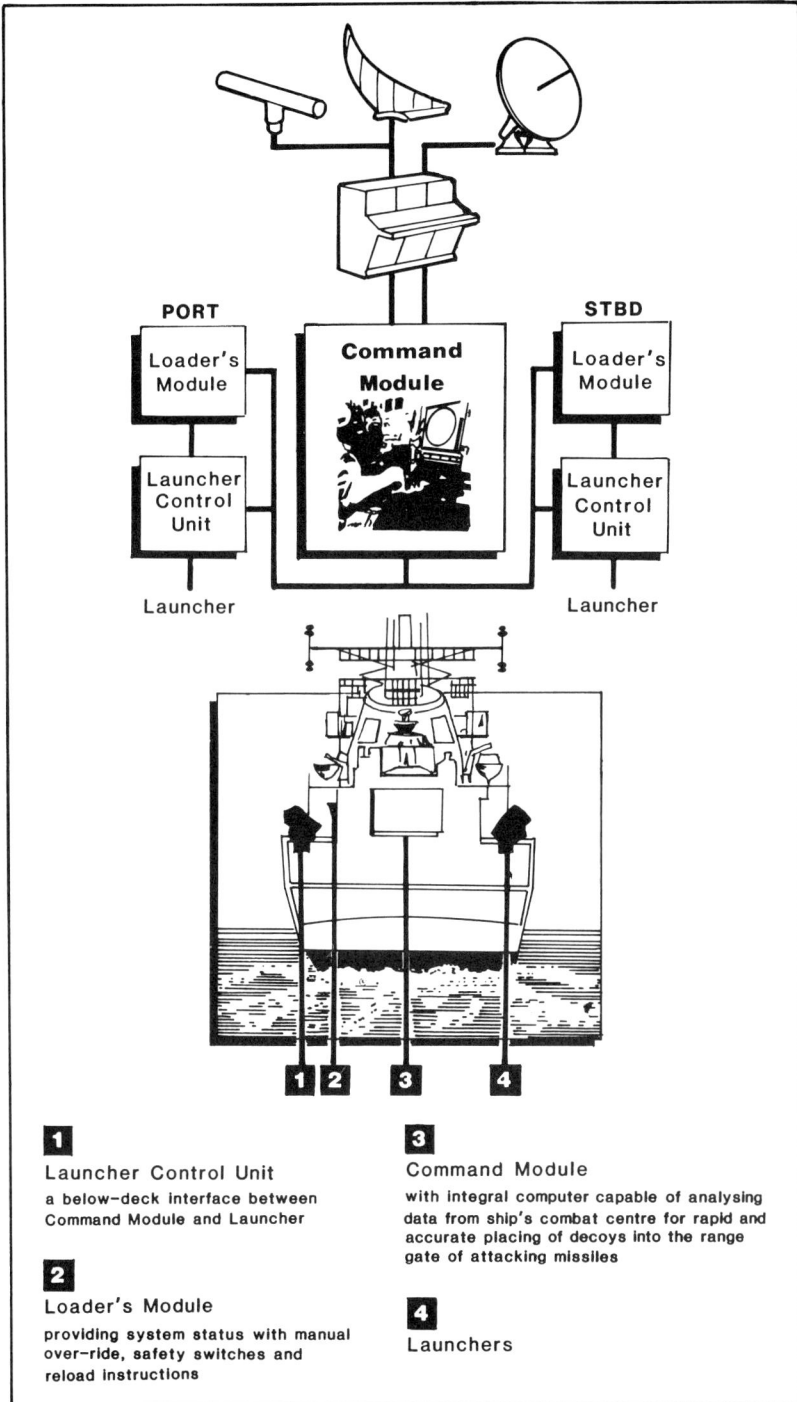

PORT

Loader's Module

Command Module

STBD

Loader's Module

Launcher Control Unit

Launcher Control Unit

Launcher

Launcher

1
Launcher Control Unit
a below-deck interface between Command Module and Launcher

2
Loader's Module
providing system status with manual over-ride, safety switches and reload instructions

3
Command Module
with integral computer capable of analysing data from ship's combat centre for rapid and accurate placing of decoys into the range gate of attacking missiles

4
Launchers

FIG. 4.5   SHIELD Decoy System *(Plessey)*

AUTO is selected, the system is set to deploy Seduction (Centroid) decoys in response to a fire instruction which accompanies the regular interface message exchange. The message will also specify which Chaff, IR, or Chaff and IR deployments are required, and supply the relevant data necessary for optimised deployment selection. The embedded tactics package is, however, structured so that should required data items be missing from the fire command message, the most probable value will be assumed in order to make the most effective response possible with limited information. The capability is provided for the return interface message to contain an advised ship manoeuvre where the computer model has shown that the available decoy response can be improved in this way.

In order that AUTO mode can react to successsive threats with a high degree of effectiveness, it is necessary that the loaded status of the launchers be monitored to ensure at least some loaded capacity for each launcher direction. Other than this, no operator intervention is necessary in the AUTO mode.

The semi-auto level of control enables the EW director to choose between Distraction and Seduction protection and retain ultimate firing control. It is also a means of retaining automatic barrel selection and fuze setting when full threat data is unavailable. In SEMI-AUTO the system selects the best Distraction or Seduction deployment according to the relative wind speed and direction. In the case of the Seduction mode, the option is provided of keying in the threat direction.

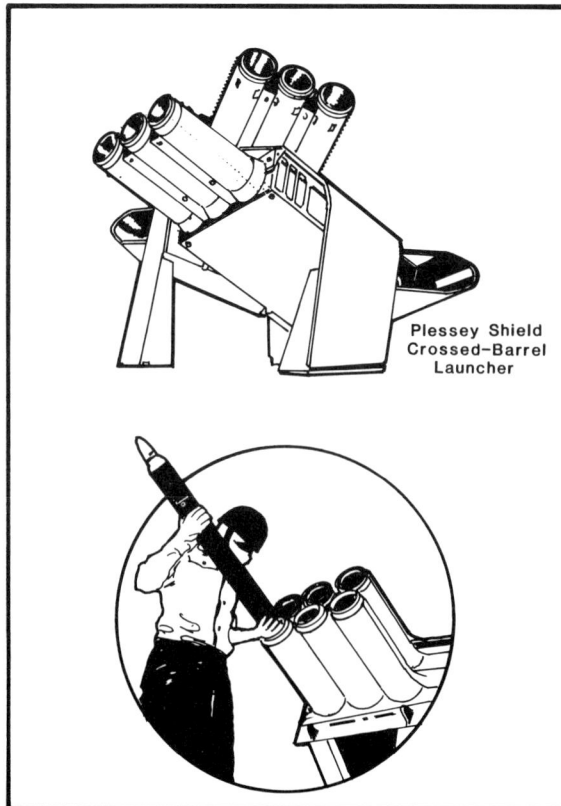

**Plessey Shield
Crossed–Barrel
Launcher**

FIG. 4.6   SHIELD Launchers and Rocket *(Plessey)*

The manual level of operation requires no interface data and can, therefore, operate in the event of any interface or sensor failure. It is also a means of implementing new deployment tactics or special trial requirements which are beyond the scope of the embedded tactical packages.

A Launcher Control Unit is required to provide an interface between the Command Module and Launcher for transmission of data. It provides all power and control signals to a launcher and it also supplies power to the Command Module and provides power conversion to DC from the ships AC supply. It provides a data bus interface with the Command Module so that the selected deployment data can be distributed and launcher status can be fed back. A loader's module adjacent to each launcher provides local control and system status.

Each launcher is an assembly of three barrel modules stacked in crossed configuration on the inclined face of a simple rugged base. A barrel module houses three stainless steel barrels with integral flow-formed helical tracks which impart spin to the decoy rockets. At the bottom of each barrel, buffer plates are provided which house inductive couplings for transmission of fuzing and firing signals. The plates are resiliently mounted to the light alloy module frame via a pair of hydro-gas shock absorbers.

The shock absorbers minimize shock loads during munition loading and also isolate the IR mortar firing loads from the launcher structure and surrounding deck, so that deck reinforcement is unnecessary. Each launcher barrel incorporates three microswitches. Two are mounted on the buffer plate and determine whether the barrel is loaded or not and the type of munition loaded (i.e. infra-red or Chaff rounds). The third switch monitors buffer plate motion and senses whether or not an IR sub-munition mortar charge has fired. If required, launcher modules can be fitted with electrical heaters for protection against icing down to −30 degress C and with self regulating control. Heating elements are set into the helical rails and around the inductive couplings. The heater harness connects to a terminal box on the launcher base. The inductive coupling and barrel status switch harnesses connect to oscillator modules which attach to one side of each module frame. The launcher base is a simple welded plate and square tube structure in light alloy which is designed for direct bolting down to levelled deck locations.

The modular design of the launchers and control equipment provides system adaptability to suit vessels of different sizes. For merchant ships, a standard ISO container is used to provide a self-sufficient SHIELD system complete with services and an operator compartment. A ship so equipped has a self-defence capability and can operate with more confidence in areas of tension or conflict. Embodying separate submunitions, the firing of the Plessey infra-red round is computer controlled and can dispense munitions at appropriate intervals. The round provides protection against the heat-seeking missile in the seduction mode.

DECOY SYSTEMS FOR SMALL WARSHIPS

For smaller vessels below the size of a frigate, simple and effective decoy systems are needed and one such is PROTEAN supplied by MEL and designed for use with their warner for locked-on missiles MATILDA. PROTEAN provides chaff and infra-red decoys which bloom in less than five seconds and produce an effective radar cross section of more than 1000 square metres.

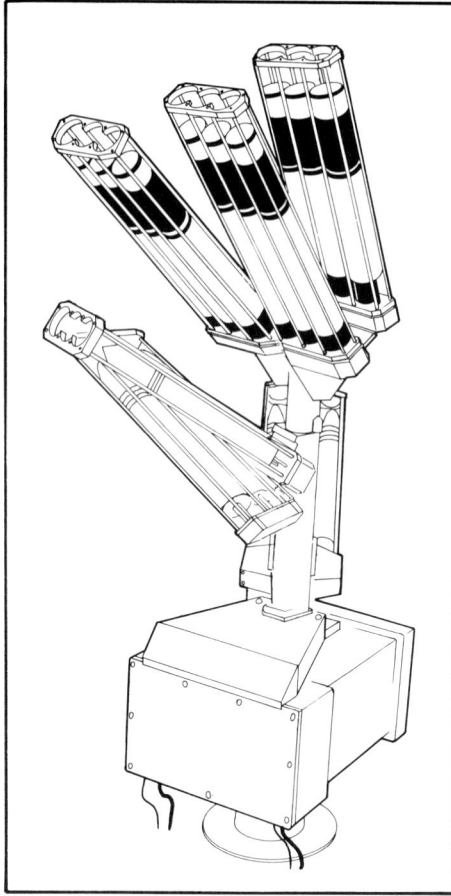

FIG. 4.7   BARRICADE Decoy Launcher *(Wallop Industries)*

PROTEAN in its basic form consists of a launcher placed on either side of the forecastle. Each launcher houses four launcher cells containing thirty-six grenades. In order to establish an effective 1000 square metre chaff cloud, nine grenades are fired in each salvo and thus each launcher is capable of developing sixteen chaff clouds before the need to reload. Reloading is accomplished by removing a spent cell and replacing it with a cell containing thirty-six grenades, the equivalent of four salvoes and the whole launcher may be reloaded in less than one minute. The chaff salvo may either be fired directly by MATILDA or by the command on receipt of a MATILDA alert.

The chaff is fired in the seduction mode. In this mode the chaff is fired into the bearing and range gate of the attacking missile's radar and the vessel is then manoeuvred to bring the chaff cloud between it and the attacking missile. The missile will then be decoyed onto the chaff cloud, whilst the vessel under attack manoeuvres out of range. The PROTEAN system can be modified to fire Infra Red flares as well as the chaff.

This combination of MATILDA and PROTEAN represents an effective and cost-effective solution for the defence of smaller vessels against sea skimming missiles. The principle of MATILDA is that it can recognize a generic type of radar rather than a specific radar and in this manner a highly cost effective solution is available. The PROTEAN launcher provides a chaff system with a very rapid response time in which the blooming time is kept below five seconds. The high manoeuvrability of the firing vessel is then made use of to move the vessel out of the missile tracking gate.

Although this is a simple concept it is very effective and simulator studies have shown that this system improves the probability of survival by 80 per cent. A course to steer computer will further aid the command in taking evasive action.

The BARRICADE radar decoy system provided by Wallop Industries uses chaff in a basically similar manner to achieve confusion, distraction and seduction but employs a greater number of small rockets rather than the larger rockets of SHIELD. The launcher has six sets of triple barrels, there is a control unit and a course-to-steer computer to assist in tactical manoeuvring as well as a ready-to-use locker for the rockets. The launcher is shown in Figure 4.7.

Parachute-borne infra-red ship decoys in the 3–5 micron and 8–14 micron wavebands are deployed from the BARRICADE Naval Decoy System, and are said to be effective against all current IR homing missiles. Development of advanced long waveband spatial IR decoys is proceeding to defeat the next generation anti-ship missile threat.

An interesting feature of BARRICADE is the provision of a white smoke screen for protection against visually aimed or homing missiles. The smoke screen is effective in some 16 seconds and its deployment from a small vessel is shown in Figure 4.8.

Wallop also provide a system known as EVADE which gives radar (chaff) and infra-red decoys for aircraft, including naval helicopters. Four lightweight scab-on dispensers (more can be added) together with a cockpit control unit make up the system, which can be adapted to suit all aircraft types. The system is easy to install and operate and the dispensers can be fitted on any suitable external surface area. Pylon-mounting is a particularly convenient method of attachment and the store carrying capacity of the pylon is not affected.

The Chaff Pack carries twenty-one cartridges which fire to the rear of the aircraft where the chaff is dispersed by the surrounding turbulence. Dipole lengths are supplied to user's requirements against a specific radar threat. The chaff is slip coated to maximise rapid blooming and minimize 'birdnesting' (i.e. individual pieces of chaff sticking together in clumps rather than dispersing).

The Flare Pack contains ten infra-red cartridges which ignite when just clear of the aircraft. Each flare has a burning time of 3 to 5 seconds. The cartridges in both Packs are ejected by electrically detonated squibs.

The various modes of operation can be pre-selected before flight or selected by the pilot during flight, as follows:

> *Single:* One chaff cloud and/or one Infra-red Flare are discharged each time the FIRE button is pressed on the Cockpit Control Unit.
> *Burst:* A series of Chaff clouds and/or Infra-red Flares.
> *Salvo:* A series of Bursts.
> *Continuous:* All Chaff and Infra-red cartridges are fired until munitions are exhausted.

The number of cartridges and time interval can be preset. When the pilot perceives a threat, by the Radar Warning Receiver or visually, he presses the FIRE button to dispense Chaff and/or Infra-red Flares accordingly.

Ignition

3 seconds

7 seconds

12 seconds

16 seconds

FIG. 4.8   BARRICADE White Smoke Screen Deployment *(Wallop Industries)*

An Advanced Decoy System

A more advanced type of off-board naval decoy is the Marconi SIREN which does not use chaff but an amplified electronic signal to attract the missile. It is fired from a rocket and is then suspended by parachute, falling slowly to the sea. It is not prone to the limitations of chaff in being recognized and discriminated against and it provides a powerful decoying signal which is equivalent to a very large decoy radar echoing area.

SIREN can also be used to control the deployment of both IR and chaff rounds.

The main system elements are:

Offboard Countermeasures Controller
Local Launch Controller
Two or Four Fixed Launchers
SIREN Countermeasures Rounds

The system is easy to install and simple to operate. SIREN is equipped with comprehensive built-in test facilities to provide ease of in-service maintenance. It can be fitted without additional deck strengthening to a wide range of ships. The system is designed to interface with existing ship sensor and control systems.

Once alerted to missile attack by the ship surveillance system the SIREN Offboard Counter-measures Controller selects the appropriate countermeasure and launcher. Unless vetoed by the Command, the system launches the SIREN countermeasures round. After firing and still within seconds of the alert, the round automatically and effectively decoys the incoming missile away from the ship.

The SIREN launcher is a 130 mm fixed structure generally implemented in banks of three to six. A standard barrel elevation angle of 45 degrees is used. The launchers require a minimum of deck space, using two positions for small ships and four for larger vessels.

The SIREN Offboard Counter-measures Controller provides the necessary interface to other ship defence systems. The unit uses its own microprocessors to determine the most suitable countermeasure, launcher and deployment position, and to initiate firing. A keyboard is provided for manual control if dictated by user requirements. The round incorporates Marconi proprietary items of advanced technology to achieve a small, lightweight, high power, low cost, expendable offboard decoy. SIREN provides a highly efficient seduction mode against radar guided missiles which is said to be more effective than chaff or onboard ECM for missile seduction. The round does not rely on active onboard ECM such as break-lock devices, for successful operation. SIREN need only be deployed after the missile is attacking the defended ship.

The main elements of the SIREN round are the low 'g' rocket, parachute, receive antenna, control electronics, and decoy electronics. After firing internal batteries provide the round with electrical power. The SIREN round is 1800 milimetres long and 130 milimetres in diameter. It has an overall mass of 28 kilogrammes and the principal parts of the round are shown in Figure 4.9.

A different and very effective type of radar decoy is the REPLICA system provided by Irvin of Great Britain Ltd. It is a rapid response, RF passive, naval decoy system giving full azimuth and elevation coverage and a broad-band response in frequency.

It consists of large corner reflectors constructed in inflatable form which float on the sea. The technique of inflation is very rapid and the design is such that, when inflated, the corner reflectors achieve the high degree of mechanical and angular accuracy

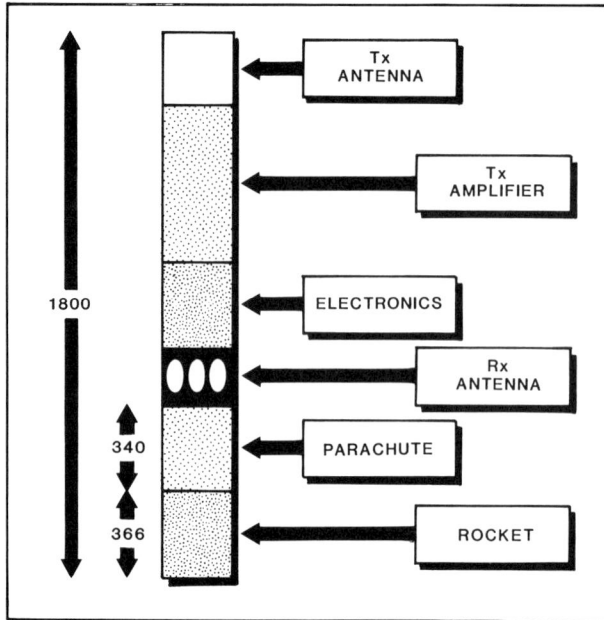

FIG. 4.9 The SIREN Decoy Round *(Marconi Defence Systems)*

necessary to provide strong reflected signals and yield a large echoing area. It is eminently suitable for the distraction and false target role and its rapid response provides significant capability in the seduction role. REPLICA is deck launched. Deployment from a ship is achieved by a simple launching cradle which can be readily fitted to all classes of ship. In its simplest form the launcher can be operated manually and thus requires no services. Remote powered operation can be provided, if required. Demands on deck space are minimal and no additional supporting underdeck structure is generally necessary.

As REPLICA is so ship-like it also makes an excellent target for training exercises, providing a 'ship' to be attacked by live air or ship-launched missiles and radar-directed guns.

Operation is fully automatic and immediate with full radar cross-section being achieved within a few seconds of hitting the sea. A remote control facility could be incorporated allowing units to be pre-seeded and then activated on command: a self-destruct facility could also be incorporated if required.

The standard REPLICA system comprises a launcher and a pair of liferaft-like containers each housing one deployable reflector unit. Being a reflector system, REPLICA gives a remarkably ship-like signature. Major advantages over chaff are claimed to have been shown by the manufacturer.

The elements of the system are shown in Figure 4.10. There appears to be no significant degree of vulnerability to discrimination by radars, and REPLICA should not be only effective against modern radars but should also provide a very large decoy signal. Its duration, or endurance as a decoy is indefinite which is a strong point in its favour.

REPLICA DEPLOYED

REPLICA ON LAUNCHER

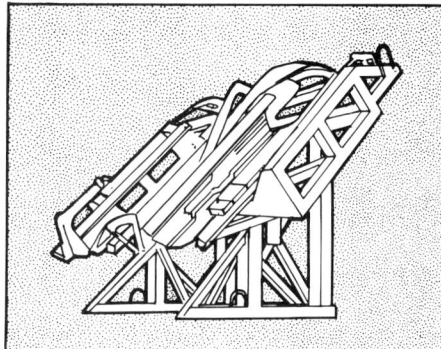

LAUNCHER

FIG. 4.10   Elements of the REPLICA Decoy *(Irvin Great Britain)*

5

Electronic Counter Counter-Measures—ECCM and Anti-Radar Measures

THE SIGNIFICANCE OF ECCM

Electronic warfare is essentially a conflict between devices which 'attack' and deceive the electronic sensors used in naval weapons, and the features in design of these sensors which make them less prone to, or immune from, electronic interference and deception. A step taken by ESM and ECM designers creates a response from ECCM designers. In this escalating battle of electronic design much ingenuity, complexity and subtlety is employed to an increasing extent because the advantages to be gained can be very significant in both tactical and cost-effectiveness terms. For obvious reasons, ECCM is the most sensitive and secret aspect of electronic warfare because to reveal the actual ECCM measures incorporated in the design of a weapon or sensor is to reveal its degree of vulnerability to ESM or ECM. Thus the discussion of ECCM which follows will be in very general terms and will deal with the types and classes of techniques which are available to electronic equipment designers. From the point of view of command and control, ECCM is really most important and the knowledge of the ECCM capability he has in his equipment will greatly influence the decisions of a commander in the way he uses his weapons and fights his ship.

ANTI-INTERCEPT MEASURES

The most obvious and basic anti-intercept measure is not to transmit, and so it is important to devise and make effective various ways to operate at sea—at least for short periods—without making radar or communications transmissions. This can be, and is, done but it certainly can create disadvantages and difficulties for the command in having no active surveillance, in navigation and station keeping and in a lack of communication with ships in company outside visual range. Nevertheless, the practice of radio silence and EMCON—emission control—is now a part of the modern methods of command and control. Judgement of when, and to what extent to use it is influenced by the tactical situation at the time and it can often be difficult to assess whether radio silence would bring a net advantage or disadvantage.

The disadvantage can be much reduced if a ship engaging in EMCON can be given surveillance information from a satellite. Here the ship only has to receive and if navigation positions and target identification are good enough it can obtain a useful picture of what is around it without using its radars. This is a feature of naval command

and control which is likely to grow in importance. While satellite sensors are essentially an important anti-intercept measure in that they enable a ship to gain information without having to transmit on their own radars, they go beyond this ECCM role in importance because they can provide very much wider spatial coverage than could a ship with only shipboard radars and ESM. Satellite sensors are discussed separately in a following section where their role in naval operations is summarised in a wider context to show them in a truer perspective.

Identification can be made difficult by the use of very short or very weak transmissions. A short burst from a radar, not regularly repeated, can be identified on an ESM equipment of high intercept probability but if it is not regularly repeated there is much less chance of its being recognized. The most distinctive feature of a radar transmission is a regular pulse repetition frequency (PRF) giving a clear musical note when intercepted. If this PRF is made noise-like through an irregular modulation the intercepted signal is much harder to recognize. If there is only one pulse per beam width in the radar signal, this is extremely difficult to recognize if it is not repeated regularly. But this type of radar modulation raises difficulties in the radar performance and so can only be used in certain suitable circumstances.

Very low signal levels in which the signal is near, or below background noise level in a normal receiver also make the task of the interceptor very difficult. But of course these low level signals also require special types of receiving techniques to make use of this form of transmission by the ship employing it. However the advantage lies with the sender, not the interceptor, as he knows precisely what type of signal is involved and can optimise the design of a receiver to accept it. Needless to say, much technical complexity is involved in this type of transmission, and it is only used for special purposes.

ANTI-JAMMING MEASURES

The prime measure to avoid jamming is frequency agility in which the radio frequency of the transmission is not stable but is caused to hop in a random fashion over a frequency band. This forces the jammer to spread his power over the band and so reduce the strength of jamming at any single frequency, or to be responsive and be able, very rapidly, to follow the hopping signal. This is difficult and results usually in the jamming suffering a loss of effectiveness. In both the transmitting equipment, be it radar or communications, and the jammer, the electronic complexity and the cost are significantly increased. A direct means of countering jamming in missile homing radars is to use it as a beacon and home to it. This is relatively easy to do and is so generally used that some modern decoys actually use noise modulation as their attracting signal in the confident expectation that missiles will automatically home to it. Various features of receiver design can be used to give a measure of immunity to jamming, such as improvements to widen the dynamic range and make saturation more difficult. These are generally useful and are normally incorporated in receivers as a matter of course and in addition to other ECCM features. While ships find noise jamming of doubtful use, it is used against ships and so anti-jamming ECCM measures are very necessary and important for naval radars and communications equipments.

ANTI-DECOY MEASURES

So important and effective are decoys in ship defence that it is not surprising to find anti-decoy techniques featuring to a major degree in missile design. Broadly, the missile must use its own programmed and designed intelligence in its homing head to be able, very quickly, to discriminate between a ship and a decoy. This it now does by using as many characteristics of the ship as it can measure and assess, such as radar echo size, temperature, the spectral aspects of the radar return and the spatial extent of the target. The modern missile uses a number of sensors, such as radar and infra-red, and a great deal of data processing to do this, and clearly much electronic complexity is involved. The sophistication and effectiveness of missile discrimination is now so advanced that simple decoys of chaff or flares may become outdated against some future designs of missile heads and new decoys require more sophistication.

The escalating response of ECCM to ECM and vice versa is particularly marked in the decoy field. It will probably continue upwards in complexity for some stages because the sea-skimming missile is such a potent naval threat and decoys are certainly the least costly method of defence against them. Under these circumstances, expenditure on both ECM and ECCM is well justified to both sides, each having much to gain or lose in a tactical sense.

ANTI-RADAR MEASURES

A number of interesting and effective measures against radar have been devised and while it is perhaps open to question whether they are rightly classified as ECCM, they are certainly very important in electronic warfare. They include the various STEALTH techniques of reducing the radar echoing area of targets, the best known of these being the use of radar absorbent material (RAM); the avoidance of distinctive radar signatures to impede recognition; and the use of the radar as a homing beacon for missiles known as anti-radar missiles (ARM). These are discussed in general terms below.

THE ANTI-RADAR MISSILE—ARM

The homing system of a missile can be designed to recognize and lock on to the signal of a ship's radar, usually a surveillance radar. In so doing it is passive, i.e. the homing head does not transmit and it cannot therefore be detected and identified by the ship's ESM equipment. The ship then has a problem in that it needs a surveillance radar to detect the attacking missile, but its radar signal is attracting the missile. Furthermore, the missile is not vulnerable to the normal radar or infra-red decoys using such measures as chaff, electronic signals and flares.

The defence against such a missile, apart from shooting it down, is to not use a shipborne surveillance radar and rely, perhaps, on satellite sensors or to employ an off-board decoy which emits the same radar signal more strongly than the actual radar sidelobes. The missile will be using the radar sidelobe signals to give it continuous homing and it is practicable to create an amplified version of this signal in the decoy. Such decoys, which must contain a considerable outfit of electronics, are expensive and, if they are to be expendable, the overall cost is quite high. The decoy must be off-board to constitute a real physical source of radiation for the missile to home to, and this means it must either float on the sea or be suspended in the air by, for example, a parachute. In both cases it would be difficult to recover and should be regarded as expendable.

A ship without active surveillance radar has, in effect, no active self-defence and is clearly at a great disadvantage. So, it can be seen that the ARM presents a nasty problem, and it is a very potent form of anti-radar measure, particularly if it is used in a mixed attack with other conventional radar guided missiles, for which the ship's surveillance radar is necessary to activate the missile defence of the ship. Once again, the ARM illustrates the vulnerability of electronic measures to exploitation—the ship's radar exploited by the ARM—and again the vulnerability of the ARM to an electronic decoy designed specially for it.

A different form of radar avoidance is found in the missile which makes no use of radar, either actively or passively, for homing and makes no use of infra-red either. This is the visually guided missile with a television camera in its nose which uses the visual image of a ship to home to. The television image is either transmitted back to the parent vehicle which launched the missile, where a human operator sees it and guides the missile accordingly, or it can be compared with a stored image of a ship in the missile's memory.

In either case, the missile is immune to decoys and one form of defence is to use a smoke screen to hide the ship. Such a smoke screening capability is provided by Wallop Industries and discussed with an illustration of its action in the earlier section on Decoys. These visually guided missiles are highly immune to all conventional decoys, and used in a mixed attack with ARM's and normal radar-guided missiles, they could further compound the problem faced by a ship in defending itself in daylight. Even at night, the use of well developed thermal imaging or image intensification techniques would give the missile a perfectly adequate visibility.

STEALTH

One aspect of EW has gained some publicity in recent years and its name, STEALTH, has become known from press and television reports. It is strictly a form of passive ECM and it is concerned with anti-radar measures; it consists of a range of techniques to reduce the radar echoing area of vehicles, mainly aircraft, missiles and ships. The reduction of the radar echoing area is important for two basic defensive reasons—it reduces the range at which the vehicles can be detected and so also the reaction time for an attack, and it makes the task of creating effective decoys easier. Indeed, if the STEALTH techniques on an aircraft or missile are well designed and it also flies low over the ground or sea, the chance of it being detected at all by radar could be very low, or it could succeed in approaching its target very closely before radars detected it. The reaction time for the target would be markedly reduced and the lethality of the attack thereby enhanced.

In the case of ships, which present very large radar targets, STEALTH techniques cannot make them invisible to radar and their principal value is to reduce the echoing area highlights and render it simpler to create decoys with a comparable or greater radar echo. Collectively, the STEALTH measures have proved to be effective and to give a very worthwhile tactical advantage. In the case of submarines where avoiding detection is paramount, the application of STEALTH techniques to periscopes and masts which have to be exposed briefly above the surface, is of value and is effective.

To reduce the radar detectability of an object it is necessary to minimise the amount of electromagnetic energy reflected back in the incident direction to the radar. Three primary methods are available to do this.

First, the material from which the target is made should have as low a reflection coefficient as is practicable or be an absorber, consistent with the structural strength required. Dielectrics and plastics are better in this respect than metals but a skin of plastic over metal would not work as the metal would reflect through the plastic skin.

Second, the target could be covered with a radar absorbent material known as RAM, which would reduce the amount of energy reflected by absorbing a good proportion of incident radar energy. This is very cost-effective for relatively small target areas, and the problems involved for the designer are to obtain a light-weight absorbent material, particularly for aircraft, and to obtain good absorption over a wide frequency range so that it is effective for a band of radar frequencies. Considerable progress has been made towards both these objectives and RAM is discussed further below.

The third method is to make the shape of the target such that it is a scatterer rather than a specular reflector which sends back a lot of electromagnetic energy in the direction from which it came. One important way to achieve this is to avoid right-angled metallic planes in the structure of the target since these constitute what are known as corner reflectors. Corner reflectors, which are simply flat sheets of metal intersecting exactly at ninety degrees, are a most effective device to create a large-echoing area and are used to enhance the visibility of buoys for navigational radar, and of meteorological balloons for radar tracking.

If the design of the ship or aircraft specifically avoids ninety degree corners, even by a few degrees, the reduction in echoing area is quite dramatic and can be several tens of decibels. Likewise, if the design of the ship or aircraft avoids large flat areas which are perpendicular to the direction of arrival of an incident radar beam, the echoing area is markedly reduced as the reflected beam is not directed back exactly in the direction of the radar. So, for example, a ship with sides which are not vertical, but inclined inwards or outwards by a few degrees, would present a smaller radar target to a sea-skimming missile homing to it by radar. Such a ship would be easier to protect by decoys, and this is very important for the very large targets presented by ships where the problem is to make a large enough decoy.

RADAR ABSORBENT MATERIAL—RAM

In Britain, work on the problem of RAM is centered in the Plessey Company and has been continuing for nearly forty years, while in Germany, work carried out by Wesch is believed to have led to a reduction in the radar signature of submarine superstructures during World War II. In the decade after the Second World War, research into Radar Absorbent Materials (RAM) continued at the Royal Signals and Radar Establishment, Malvern (known then as the Telecommunications Research Establishment) and the Royal Aircraft Establishment, Farnborough in the UK.

Although real progress was made with these research programmes, few practical applications resulted despite the fact that the transition from laboratory results to practical materials had been achieved. In this respect Britain appeared to establish a lead, although the secret nature of the work resulted in a fragmentary approach to research into 'low observables'.

American interest in STEALTH technology has centred on aircraft and missiles and the reduction of the Rockwell B-1B's radar signature (said to be ten times less than the externally similar B-1A) is a notable achievement by any standards. Meanwhile, all major US airframes manufacturers are engaged on low observable programmes both for new and current aircraft.

Advances in this field are by no means limited to Western nations. It is likely that the Soviet Army employs RAM screens on armoured vehicles, as the most advanced published texts on the subjects are from Russian authors. As a modern main battle tank can cost over one million pounds, the comparatively small sum necessary to reduce its radar signature would seem to be money well spent, not least because of the new generation of 'intellient' munitions being developed by NATO to provide a 'top attack' capability.

The experience of modern anti-ship missiles in the Falklands conflict served to focus the attention of naval commanders on the opportunities for deploying radar camouflage materials on surface ships. It was originally considered that surface ships possessed too high a radar signature to allow any measure of suppression, but the value of selective treatment has been demonstrated very effectively.

Just as selected application of RAM to a ship can result in a significant reduction in its radar cross section, (RCS), so too can the RCS of an aircraft be reduced by the judicious installation of suitable materials. Certain parts of an aircraft are large scattering centres of radar energy; these areas are readily identifiable on any current aircraft and can be treated with appropriate material.

In developing RAM for military applications it has not been enough to produce laboratory effective devices; most applications require a microwave absorber which is of negligible weight and thickness, suitable for application to any complex structure and which performs efficiently over a wide range of frequencies. The physical properties of existing materials prevent the complete combination of these objectives. Thus a number of magnetic, dielectric and magnetic-dielectric materials are used to obtain a low reflection under specific conditions. By controlling the material type and thickness, loss factor and surface impedence, performance can be peaked at a single frequency, multiple frequencies or over a broad band. Basically, the materials fall into one or two categories: resonant and non-resonant.

Resonant materials rely both on the attentuation of the incident wave and on the interference effect produced by the reflection from their backings. Based upon flat polymeric sheet material, they have many applications where thickness and environmental robustness are critical. Resonant materials divide into three classes, namely solid magnetically loaded, solid dielectric loaded and sandwich type absorbers. The most simple example of these materials is the Quarter Wave absorber in which a reflector-backed lossy material is tuned to give a single resonant response.

In theory, it is possible to design these materials to resonate at any frequency in the radar bands, to give limited frequency cover or to design a multiple layer system for resonance at multiple frequencies, to give broadband characteristics. Practical limitations of weight in the case of longer wavelengths, or of control of material thickness at the shorter millimetric wavelength, and environmental conditions, such as humidity, temperature or contamination, are limiting factors which must be taken into consideration in the selection of appropriate material for each application. The majority of resonant absorbers were originally designed to offer optimum performance at normal incidence. It is now more usual to specify a designated polarization to extend the range of absorbers offered to give absorption at any specified angle of incidence.

Resonant absorbers are available in single layer or multiple layer form and as flat sheets, or moulded to accommodate complex shapes when superior adhesion or rapid fitting is required. The base material for the dielectric or magnetically lossy ingredients can be specified from a range of polymeric materials. The absorbers are optimised for high performance (25dB or 99.7 per cent absorption) at the design frequency, polarization and angle of incidence. The use of multiple layer material can provide a broadband performance, particularly at the higher frequencies.

Fig. 5.1   Plessey LA–O Flexible Non-resonant Absorber (*Plessey*)

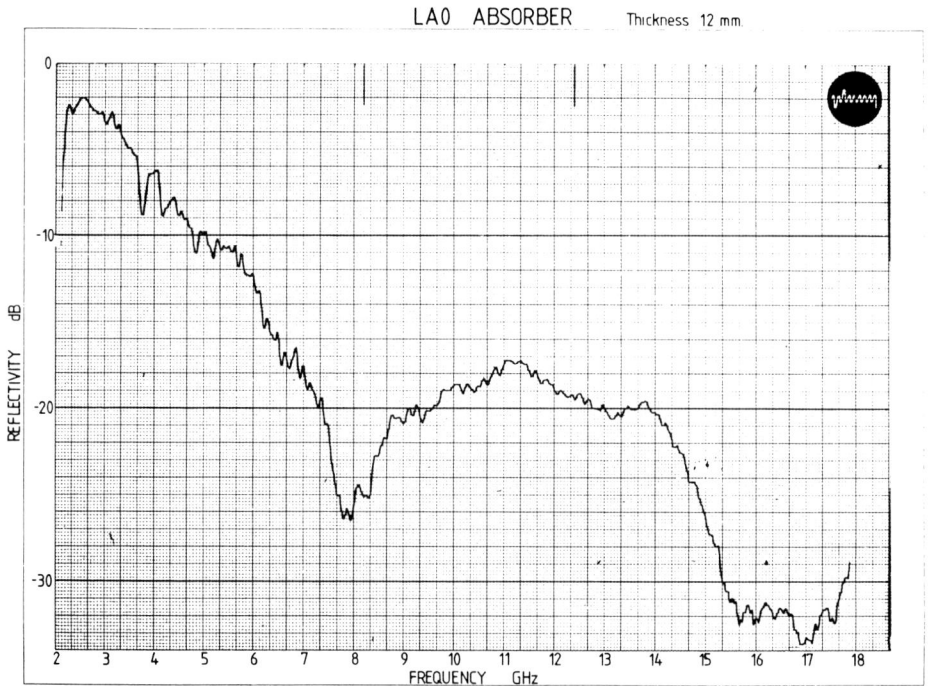

Fig. 5.2   LA–O Absorption Characteristics (*Plessey*)

Non-resonant absorbers, which work on the principle of presenting graded dielectrically lossy material to incident microwave energy, are available in a wide variety of forms. A diverse set of materials is based on open cell foams, non-metallic meshes and honeycombs, where the graded loss is achieved by an exponential distribution of the lossy ingredient from the front to the rear surface.

Many of the RAM materials can be filled with rigid microwave transparent materials to produce absorbers with structural properties. The use of such rigid radar transparencies as polyurethane, polypropylene or syntactic foams allows absorbers to be integrated into the fabric of components and structures. Honeycomb treated as an absorber can be skinned on the front and rear surfaces with suitable composites to produce a rigid material suited to airframe applications.

At millimetric frequencies, physically profiled elastomers offer a practical solution to the problem of providing broad-band performance in a harsh environment. The thickness of the absorber need only be a few millimetres and the base material can be chosen from a range of proven elastomers used for resonant absorbers.

An important feature of non-resonant materials is that they absorb radar energy across a wide range of frequencies and are sometimes referred to as broad-band absorbers.

The ultimate conclusion of RAM technology must be a 'DC to Daylight' multispectral absorber of infinitesimal weight and low cost. Along the way, materials are being produced which absorb radar energy and provide infra-red signature reduction.

High temperature materials are under investigation, and considerable research effort would be required to combine the conflicting design criteria for radar absorbing and IR emissivity control into one to produce a readily applied medium. Radar absorbent paints are feasible for high performance in the millimetric bands, where the absorbing layer is less than 1 mm in thickness. More work is required on the concept of structural RAM for vehicle construction: lightweight for airframes, and anti-ballistic (i.e. proof against shrapnel) for ships. With such materials new weapons platforms could be designed from the onset with very low radar signatures.

Reference is often made to the radar cross section (RCS) or radar signature of potential targets. The terms are usually interchanged in the literature and they are applicable to any vehicle or installation which can be detected by radar. The RCS or radar signature indicates the expected level of energy in radar returns and it contains characteristics which enable signal processing to be employed on the received signal for target identification.

Except where a very low radar signature is the main design criterion, in RPVs and missiles for example, radar cross section reduction (RCSR) cannot achieve total camouflage against dedicated surveillance radars. However, a modest reduction in RCS of 12dBs (93.7 per cent) reduces the radar detection range in free space by half. Increasingly, reduction of radar signatures is being viewed as an integral part of electronic countermeasures.

For the same jamming effectiveness, the jammer power to screen a vehicle can be reduced in direct proportion to the RCS or, in other words, if a particular burn-through range can be tolerated and the RCS of the host vehicle can be reduced by as little as 10dB then the effective power requirement of an active ECM equipment can be reduced by 90

FIG. 5.3   Plessey LA–1 Structural Non-resonant Absorber (*Plessey*)

per cent. Similarly, when chaff is employed to protect a target, a reduction in the RCS of the target by 10dB (90 per cent) allows the quantity of chaff to be reduced by 90 per cent.

In the naval scenario, protection can be afforded to surface vessels which operate jamming systems against anti-ship missiles. The power difference between on-board and off-board jammers in a helicopter is usually a factor of 10, hence for a vessel with a nominal RCSR of 10dB (90 per cent), the helicopter system provides the same level of screening as does an on-board jammer for an untreated ship.

The theoretical analysis of radar signatures is an extremely complex subject and research continues into the mathematical concepts. Scale models have been used for some time in an attempt to measure the RCS of full size aircraft and ships but it has been

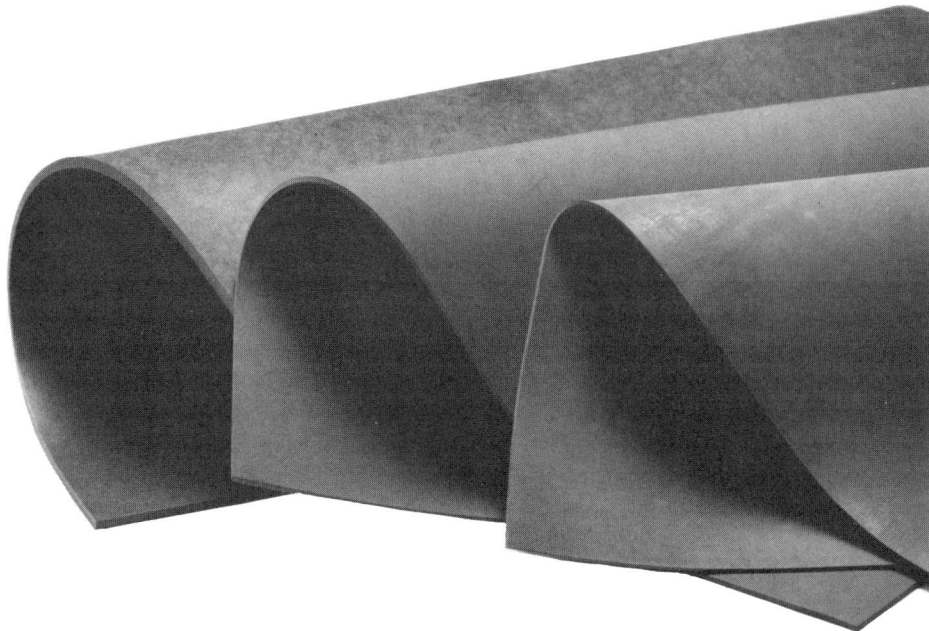

FIG. 5.4   Plessey Resonant Polymer Sheet RAM (*Plessey*)

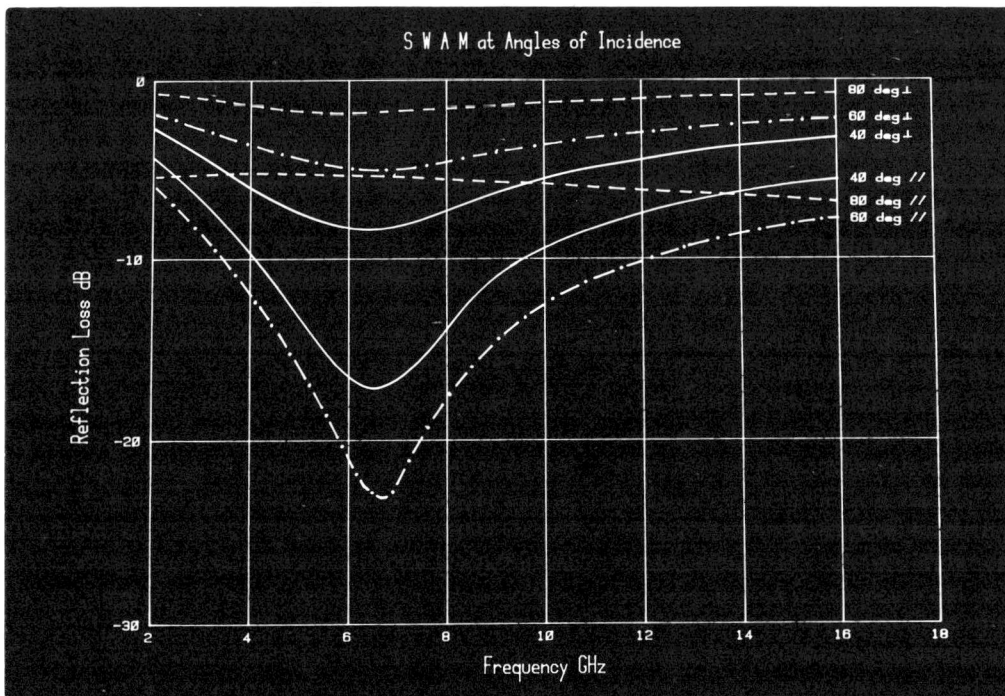

FIG. 5.5   Absorption Characteristics of Resonant Polymer RAM (*Plessey*)

shown that unless the model is a perfect replica, with every cavity and rivet head reproduced, then the results can be very misleading. It is clearly desirable, where possible, to measure actual ships and aircraft if a radar signature reduction exercise is to be undertaken, but the composition of a radar echo can be difficult to interpret correctly. A radar signature is comprised of an array of elemental signals returned from the so called 'scattering centres' on a body which are formed from dihedral and trihedral corners and re-entrant cavities. The strongest signal elements are defined as emanating from the primary scattering centres, and the remaining signals are returned from the secondary centres. Other secondary effects, such as surface waves, also contribute to a radar signature.

For first efforts in radar cross section reduction, the primary vehicle features are treated first. For radar signature reduction, the scattering centres are suppressed through the application of RAM or shaping in an iterative fashion with measurements taken at each stage to identify the next most significant set of scattering centres. Progression is then made through the secondary effects.

An interesting example of a secondary effect is the contribution made to a radar signature by surface waves. Specular radiation coming in contact with a conducting surface will generate not only a reflection, but also a small current travelling parallel to

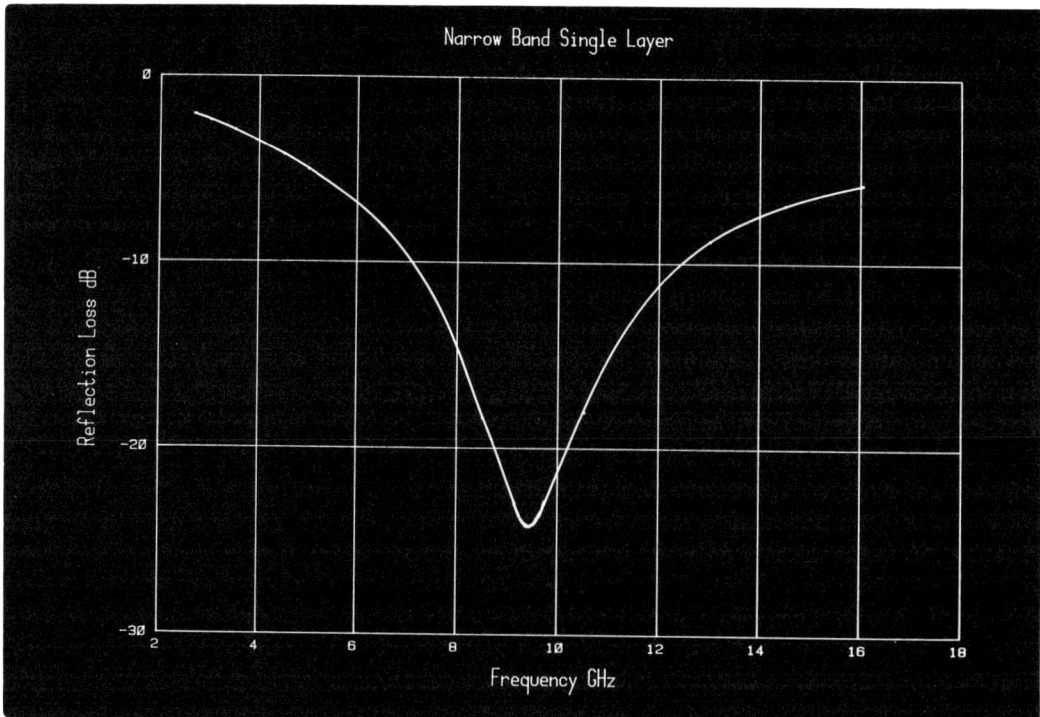

FIG. 5.6   Absorption Characteristics of SWAM—Resonant Absorber for High Angles of Incidence (*Plessey*)

the conductor's surface; this condition is known as a surface or travelling wave. The surface wave will continue along the conductor's surface until it reaches a discontinuity or a change in the shape of the surface. A surface wave will be reflected from a discontinuity and it will leave a conductor along a curved plane to become an electromagentic wave in free space.

In a typical case of radar energy incident on the leading edge of an aircraft wing, a surface wave is set up on the wing which travels to the discontinuity of the edge of an access panel. The wave is reflected from the panel edge back to the leading edge. As the wave encounters the curved surface, it leaves the conductor to re-radiate as an EM wave, and this can be detected as a return by the illuminating radar. A thin magnetic RAM coating applied on the conducting surface is very effective in reducing returns from such surface waves.

Returns from surface waves are generally only significant at low levels of radar signature and they are suppressed along with other secondary scattering centres in highly 'stealthed' vehicles once the main scatters have been removed from the overall signature. Vehicles with very large signatures such as ships cannot use RAM to make them invisible to radar. However, the use of RAM to reduce their cross-section provides two advantages; as part of an ECM suite it enhances the use of both chaff and jammers which increases survivability; it also disguises the vehicle, for example, a large ship can be made to appear as a smaller or completely different class of ship to enemy radar.

Another type of radar cross-section reduction lies in the form of tactical concealment by the use of camouflage screens and netting. These generally provide for radar, visual and even IR camouflage. They must be light, flexible and environmentally tough. Very wide broadband performance is usually required for counter-surveillance measures. The use of RAM in netting form allows large vulnerable assets and fixed installations to be screened from radar surveillance and radar guided weapons.

Selective use of RAM at optimum locations on vehicles or ships can pay off with valuable RCS reduction benefits. It has been proved conclusively that a vehicle's radar signature can be significantly reduced or changed in operational terms with careful and selective use of RAM where a total covering would be impractical. Target acquisition by some missiles will depend upon target signature identification techniques rather than simple detection to avoid the possibility of attacking low value false targets and decoys. It has been shown that the radar signature can be modified and hence achieve deception of acquisition.

It is relatively straightforward to produce radar absorbing materials from aramid or some other composite material to provide anti-ballistic or armour protection. However, this would be more effective if planned in the design of a vehicle from the outset. Combat helicopters also lend themselves to the use of lightweight RAM as an integral part of their structure. The weight penalty would not be significant and the level of survivability in the combat zone could be increased considerably. It is certainly feasible for long range stand-off or 'cruise' missiles to be produced with the entire airframe manufactured from absorbent materials, thereby reducing their radar signatures to very low levels. Composite RAM can be incorporated in fixed-wing aircraft, but this too is only really feasible if consideration were to be given at the design stage.

A vitally important aspect of RAM, when applied in the military environment, is that, unlike conventional ECM, it is entirely passive. It is a 'fit and forget' system and is virtually maintenance free.

OTHER ASPECTS OF STEALTH

The interesting point in this subject of STEALTH is that electronic warfare is now so important in its contribution to the effectiveness of defence against modern weapons and sensors that it influences the basic architecture of ships and aircraft. It is considered as a primary factor in the initial design concepts of these vehicles and this fact is testimony to both the influence of EW in modern warfare and to the effectiveness of STEALTH measures. The Type 23 frigate is the first Royal Navy design of warship to include STEALTH techniques, and their application to aircraft design in the United States has been reported in the media.

Measures to avoid detection are not confined to anti-radar techniques. Steps are taken in ships to make them less easy to detect by simple infra-red sensors using elements which respond to the high temperature end of the IR spectrum. A single hot spot, such as a flare or a hot funnel, is much easier to detect than a large warm target, such as the hull of a ship. So consideration is given in ship design to provide cooling for funnels, or to screen hot parts of funnels from the direct view of homing missiles. This increases the task of the missile designer and forces him to employ more sophisticated IR detectors which are responsive to lower temperatures and attempt to discriminate in favour of large spatial target and against point-source decoys.

Submarines use absorbing panels or tiles on their hulls to absorb the energy from active sonar transmissions and so reduce their echoing area to this sensor. However, while STEALTH measures give success against radar, infra-red and sound waves it is much more difficult to achieve a similar success against optical and visual sensors. Missiles and surveillance sensors which use the visible part of the electromagnetic spectrum in, for example, television homing and photo-reconnaissance are not susceptible to reduction of echoing area techniques. Their *modus operandi* is based on detailed target recognition and only clouds or smoke screens offer a means of concealment.

A rather different manifestation of the principles of STEALTH lies in avoiding recognition, if the total avoidance of detection is impractical.

Tactically one of the most important functions of electronic warfare is the provision of information on target identity. With this, the entire threat appreciation is greatly aided and the allocation and deployment of weapons can be considered and planned. It is obtained because many military radars have distinctive signatures in their set of characteristics of frequency, PRF, pulse width and aerial rotation rate which arises because they were designed only for optimum performance without consideration of their signature. There is therefore tactical merit in designing equipment to have transmission characteristics which are as non-distinctive as possible to avoid revealing its identity.

For example, warships use for navigation and helicopter direction civil marine radars which have a signature identical to that given by merchant ships using the same radars. This is a useful means of radar concealment of identity, especially in periods of tension and limited war situations. Also, consideration is now given in weapon and surveillance radar design to radar signatures which will not immediately identify a warship. It is quite a change from past practices when only the maximum radar performance was the factor which governed the form of the signal, and as a consequence the old RN Type 984 radar instantly identified an aircraft carrier to ESM equipment in aircraft on ships.

This is another example of EW considerations causing a profound influence on basic design at the earliest conceptual stages of an equipment, and it illustrates again the deep significance of this branch of naval warfare. Some thirty years ago it would have been quite unthinkable that the shapes of ships' hulls and the form of a radar or communications transmission would be influenced to any degree by EW considerations. Even the early naval EW enthusiasts would be astonished at the depth to which EW has now penetrated into the fabric of tactics and the early design of ships, aircraft and weapon systems.

SATELLITE SENSORS

A satellite sensor using photography, infra-red imagery, radar or ESM can be very valuable to a ship at sea for two main reasons. The first advantage is that it can give very extensive spatial coverage whether it be an orbiting or a geostationary satellite, and it can observe an area of sea and airspace around the ship which is much greater than that which could be achieved by the ship's horizon-limited sensors. Of course it may be weather-limited for operation of photography and infra-red imagery due to the presence of clouds and mist, but it would not be weather limited for radar and ESM. The visual detail in photography and infra-red images would contribute significantly to determining the identity of targets, and ESM signal analysis will provide information probably much more rapidly on target identity if the targets are transmitting.

The information from the reconnaissance satellite would be passed to the ship either directly or indirectly through a ground station, depending on where the satellite data is analysed and interpreted. By this means very early warning of a threat may be obtained and a commander at sea may obtain a comprehensive surface and air picture of the situation around his ship or force. The second advantage is that all this information can be obtained without the ship or force transmitting from any of its own sensors and so revealing its presence and identity. Of course this advantage is only complete if the enemy is not also using reconnaissance satellites. In this case it also could detect the naval force, though its ESM might have more difficulty in identifying a silent ship. However, in general, with the function of sensors being provided by reconnaissance satellites, ships can now be regarded more as weapon carriers and, provided that the satellite information is good enough, only needing to use their own sensors in the final stages of an approach to an attack. This changes the tactics of the warship, but not its basic purpose. It does not permit any reduction in the sensor fit of a ship as the provision of satellite sensor information can only at present be regarded as a valuable bonus when it is available, and not as a replacement for a ship's own sensors.

Satellite reconnaissance may be regarded as the ultimate stage of airborne early warning and it is probably the latest and most significant new capability in naval sensors. It does have difficult technical problems on many occasions because its very extensive field of view brings in a very great deal of information which must be processed, examined and assessed as to its tactical significance. While this process is much aided by computer techniques, it is still a very significant task and will inevitably cause some delay between detection of an object or signal and the report reaching the ship on what it is believed to be. Nevertheless, satellite reconnaissance is now being more widely used for both civil and military purposes and ships at sea are likely to benefit increasingly from it as data handling techniques become more powerful.

Satellite-borne radar is, to a degree, prone to confusion from ECM. Jamming and false target generation will certainly impede a satellite radar to some extent depending upon its design, and they may well be more effective in deceiving a machine than a man. A human operator can make adjustments to controls and see more through ECM measures than an automatic detector, so ECM against this type of surveillance could be beneficial to the ships at sea. It will always be a command decision on whether the tactical advantages outweigh the disadvantages in using ECM, and this applies equally to its use against distant spacecraft employed by an enemy. There is no dogma to assist the process of command and control in making decisions of this type; each tactical situation must be assessed in its own circumstances. It must be decided, as an item of ship fitting policy, whether or not to invest in ECM equipment for use against satellite reconnaissance and this also requires good judgement in selecting a ship's overall weapon system.

It is interesting that satellites are being used increasingly for civil marine purposes also. They are employed for communication, and a service is provided by the INMARSAT organization which can also be used for merchant ships automatically to report their position. Satellite sensors using infra-red and visible photography are used to survey and measure land resources such as the distribution of crops. The entire field of satellite sensoring has a large civil impetus behind it and it is rapidly becoming a normal, possibly the prime method of monitoring large areas of the earth's surface. The naval application is therefore no more than one other use of an established new technical capability.

6

Operational Aspects of Electronic Warfare

Success in naval electronic warfare is not governed entirely by the type and performance of the equipment fitted in the ship, but is much influenced by how it is used tactically and by how the information it produces is interpreted. Thus, the professional naval and the tactical skill of the command in a ship is an important ingredient in EW success, and the total EW function is a contribution of human expertise and equipment performance.

For this reason, the Royal Navy has initiated a specialist EW Branch and provides specific training and teaching in the art and practice of electronic warfare. For example, the types of question which must be addressed by Naval Officers at sea are where, and for how long, to use emission control (EMCON) and refrain from using active sensors for detection and communication, and when to use ECM in addition to, or in place of, defence weapons such as guns and missiles. These questions, and others, are studied at the Maritime Tactical School and they involve some complex considerations of relative advantages and disadvantages of the EW options in naval tactics.

A ship proceeding silently, not using its active sensors, may not detect another ship or aircraft which is also proceeding silently and so is not detected by ESM. A ship using its active sensors may give an advantage to an enemy using ESM alone. To use ECM measures and the ship's own weapons may be a disadvantage, since the ECM measures may adversely affect the ship's weapons and sensors. Radio transmissions can be intercepted by the enemy as well as the intended recipient. This opens communications channels that are not crypto-protected to eavesdropping, and other radio transmissions, such as radar, to electronic analysis which can reveal the signature of the radiating equipment and thus compromise the identity of the parent ship or aircraft. Transmissions can also be DF'd which will disclose the position of the source.

The degree of risk and the range at which such techniques can be used will vary with frequency and power, but the dependence of modern naval forces on the use of communications and electronics for the development of full fighting potential exposes them to enemy use of electronic warfare, of which these activities are part. The intended policy for the control of electronic emissions, EMCON, is therefore a central feature of any operational plan, because any restriction on radio or radar will reduce fighting efficiency in some measure.

All these questions, and others, have to be seen in the light of individual tactical situations and be weighed up accordingly; there are few simple rules which govern all situations. The net result is that, to a large extent, electronic warfare can be as successful as the skill of the command and the performance of the equipment permit, and the contribution of the man can be as important as that of the machine. A man-machine mix of this nature, involving judgement and training, is an essential feature of EW, and the fact that this was recognized and provided for by the Royal Navy from the earliest days of EW is a basic reason why EW has been so successful in British naval circles.

This recognition of the essential nature of EW extends also to the choice and design of equipment and has forged a particularly close link between EW equipment designers and naval users. And this, in turn, is one important reason why British naval EW equipment is so effective at sea. Naval Application Officers, who are users and maintainers of EW (and other) equipment maintain a close dialogue with EW equipment designers in both Ministry of Defence and industrial laboratories from the earliest stages of a project and they ensure that the special features and characteristics of equipment required for naval use at sea are known to the civilian designers. The Application Officers behave as 'Expert Users', not as engineering designers, and the unique contribution they make is most valuable. This excellent form of user participation in equipment design is unique to the Royal Navy and is not employed by the other two Services. All these factors contribute to what may be termed the 'operational pedigree' of British naval EW equipment and to the Royal Navy's practice of EW at sea. British industry has drawn benefit from this situation in that the EW equipment it offers on the world market is recognized as being very well founded and the cachet in selling EW equipment actually used by the RN is very important in exporting. While operational considerations are relevant to all naval weapons and sensors, they are particularly relevant in electronic warfare and the treatment of EW within the overall fabric of naval command and control involves rather special tactical education where the Royal Navy has been singularly successful in its procedures.

ELECTRONIC WARFARE SIMULATION

Modern electronic warfare equipment is increasingly important in naval combat and it is generally complex and sophisticated. It involves, in most cases, the use of a skilled operator to interpret the information on the EW displays and process it selectively as part of the overall command and control function in the ship. Training and experience are very necessary to produce the required level of skill in operators and, since it is difficult and expensive to train operators in realistic naval exercises at sea, there has grown up a sophisticated and very effective use of electronic warfare simulators. The design, deployment and tactical use of enemy systems and their use of the electromagnetic spectrum is usually classified, as is the knowledge of one's own electronic countermeasures. This means that covert simulation of electromagnetic combat conditions is a practical economic method of ensuring effective combat readiness with validated EW systems and tactics.

Usually a software-based simulator is employed to gain flexibility in making changes in the environment of emissions which is being represented and a processor, of adequate capacity, is used to provide a comprehensive digital model of the electromagnetic environment. The digital model is able to describe each real time change in that environment so that it can produce a digital emission description of each new element (i.e. pulse). In addition, a facility for higher level control allows real time alteration of the elemental emissions to represent tactically variable combat conditions. The digital descriptor information is used to control the real time generation of RF signals, for direct injection into the EW receiving equipment. An alternative to cable coupling with

DF antenna simulation is the use of radiated RF in an anechoic chamber, which is a less favoured, though at times necessary, higher cost approach. Although it is now possible to represent most practical conditions using 'indoor trials simulations' it is still necessary to have a means of verifying the simulation. For this reason the ability to recreate, in a cost effective manner, simple test conditions on EW trials ranges using EW environment simulators is a necessary feature of modern, in depth operational EW support.

If the simulator is to be used to stimulate the prime EW equipment via some form of EM coupling (cable or anechoic chamber), and that equipment has processor(s) and human(s) in the loop, then all the characteristics of the environment that change with time must be represented at the rates of change that occur naturally. Further, if the EW system or the human is able to make a tactical response, e.g. alter the position of the platform, counter a weapon, change an element of the environment or introduce or delete targets, then these real time events should dynamically, within the correct response time, alter the simulated environment. For these reasons, the simulation must truly operate in real time in order to provide a detailed representation of both electromagnetic and combat conditions.

Radars employ a wide variety of beam shapes and volume scanning patterns to perform various surveillance and tracking tasks. The EW receiver observes these as gross amplitude modulation of the radar's prime modulation characteristic, i.e. the pulse train. The scan amplitude modulation is a function of

Motion of the beam
The three dimensional gain profiles of the beam and
The relative position of the emitter with respect to the EW receiver.

Accurate modelling of this characteristic is extremely important as it determines the number of pulses above the receiver's threshold that are received and therefore has a direct bearing on the likely EW system's response time.

The basis of modelling the scan modulation is the model of the gain of the antenna in azimuth and elevation. In general, the antenna gain is either a pencil beam shape or fan beam, although with certain multiple mode radars, the antenna may produce a set of gain profiles.

Weapon emissions have extremely complex EM signatures and interactively relate to the engagement of a target by the weapon. Characteristically, these emissions relate to three prime weapon states: Early Warning/Surveillance/Identification; Tracking and Guidance. The initiation timings and the associated emission characteristics at each stage of the weapon's engagement of the target will be governed by the weapon's combat logic, tactical command and control and the track of the target. A generalized event or weapon state software model allows the user to create the separate emitter or radar sets necessary to replicate the emissions associated with each state. Using this generalized software framework, the user may construct specific weapons by entering values for use by the generalized control logic which provides for the surveillance state to initiate tracking or guidance automatically.

A further element of complexity is the influence of terrain on the propagation of radio waves. For ground based microwave emitters, the field strength decreases very dramatically if line of sight does not exist. Thus, it is important to model this to obtain an indication of the true emission density and the consequential loss of data that an ESM

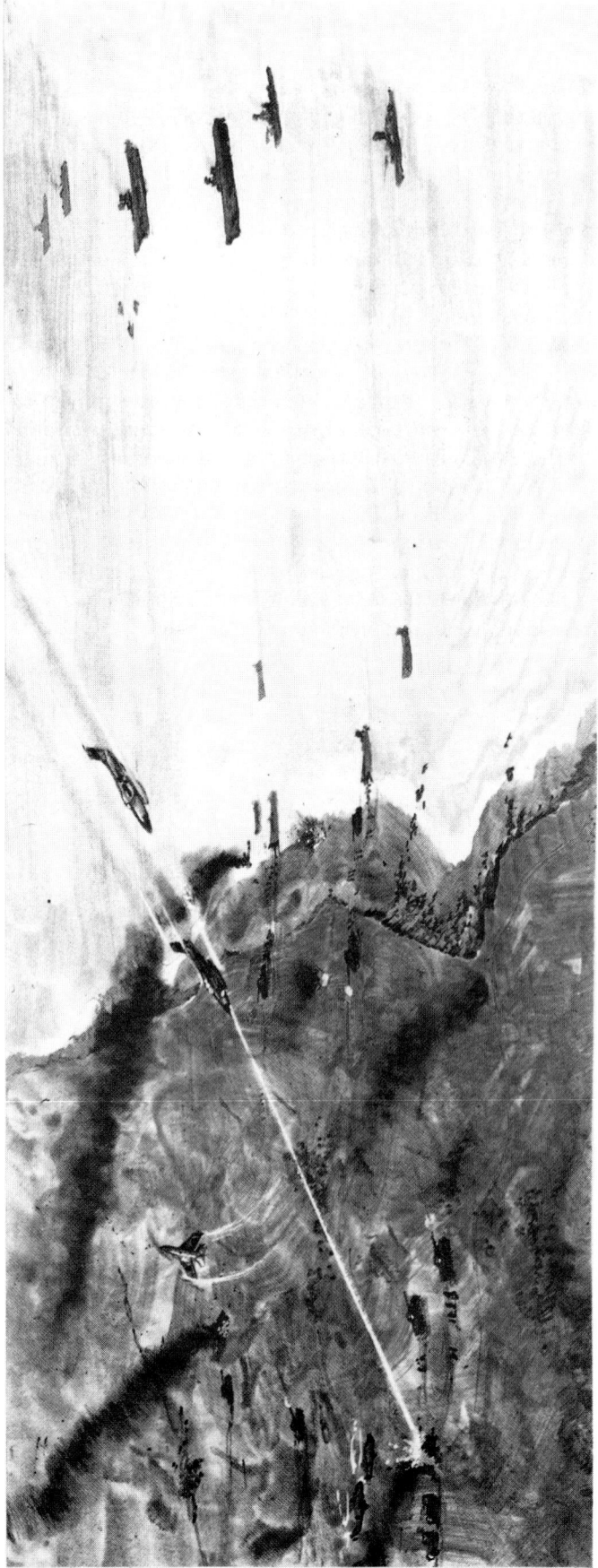

FIG. 6.1   Real Life Situation for Simulation   *(British Aerospace)*

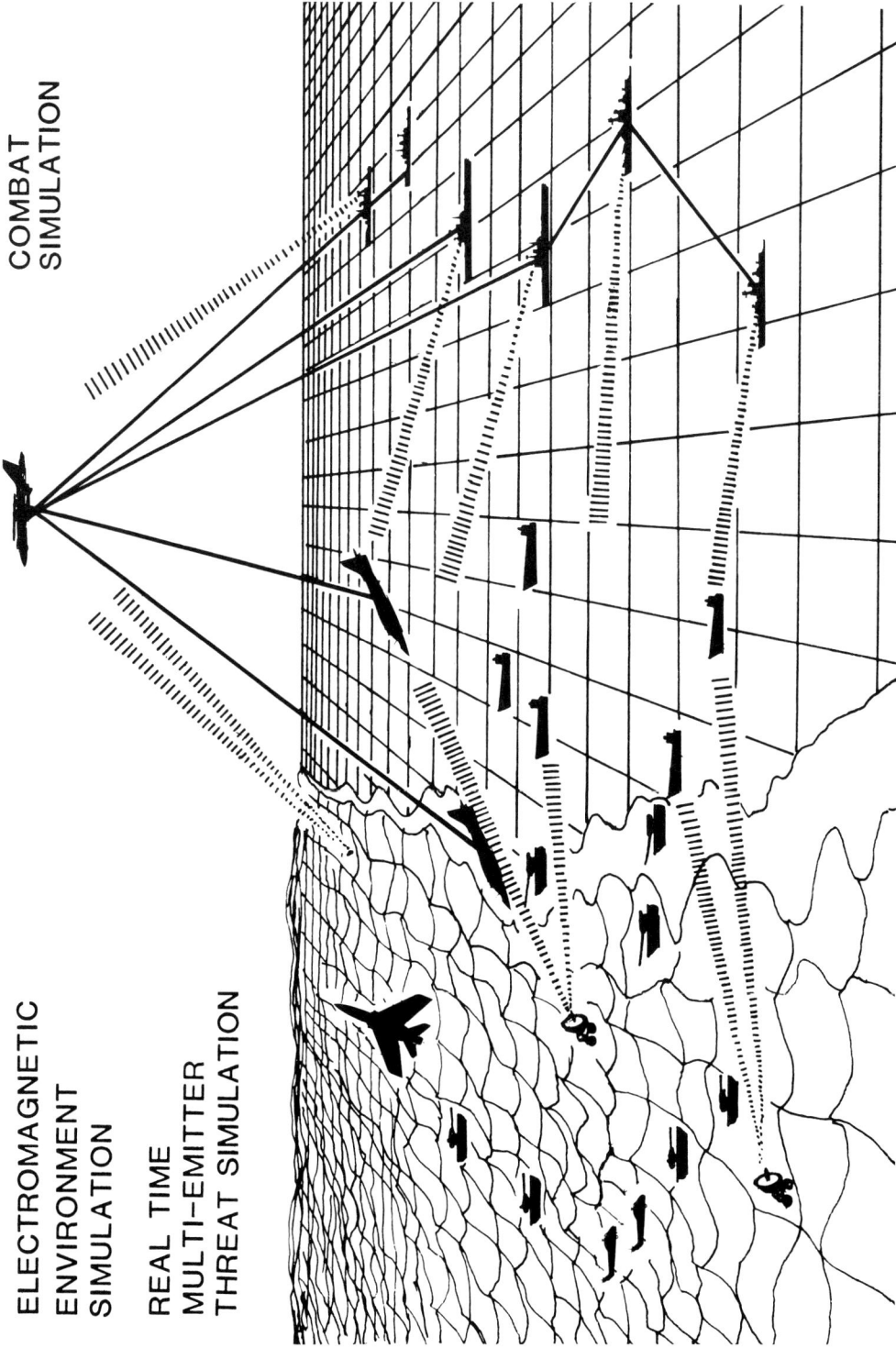

COMBAT
SIMULATION

ELECTROMAGNETIC
ENVIRONMENT
SIMULATION

REAL TIME
MULTI-EMITTER
THREAT SIMULATION

FIG. 6.2 Combat Simulation *(British Aerospace)*

system will experience at different altitudes. Digital terrain maps are in use with simulators and automatic software is used to compute the first order line of sight terrain effects. In addition, more comprehensive terrain profile propagation prediction methods may be used to compute the predicted field strength which may be used with the emitter models to select in real time the received field strength.

Within the range of over land and maritime scenarios, the propagation of radio energy is influenced in a number of important ways; the general influence of range between the receiver and emitter, terrain obstructions, multipath conditions in the land/sea environment and anomalous propagation conditions. Depending on the scenario, each of these effects may be incorporated as additional models that control the basic emitter model.

Simulators based on these principles can be used to inject simulated signals into the actual EW equipment which the operator is being trained to use. He sits at the display and is given a presentation of data similar to that which he would see in actual operations at sea. Enormous complexity of software and hardware is involved in creating a realistic picture, and the results are most impressive. Very realistic training is achieved. Alternatively, the simulator can be an entirely separate equipment not attached to the actual EW equipment for which the operator is being trained. The simulator is then known as an 'equipment mimic' and it performs the same function of creating a realistic display of signals for operator training.

Analysis of threat signal structures and their correlation with intelligence data is fundamental to the practice of electronic warfare. For this reason, training in threat signal recognition is a basic requirement for all service personnel actively engaged in the practice of EW. This basic training needs to be supplemented with practical exercises and the use of a Basic Emitter Analysis Trainer which provides a cost effective solution. This trainer may be configured to be a video signal generator, or an equipment mimic, with representative displays and controls.

Advanced signal recognition techniques associated with ELINT depends on a detailed examination of the fine RF signal structure plus any associated signals. To train ELINT operators in advanced signal analysis and situation awareness effectively, a high fidelity RF threat signal generator is needed to stimulate the ELINT system. Simulator equipments meet these requirements. In addition, the equipment provides the basis for ELINT equipment maintenance and the development of additional measurement processes.

Just as flight simulators have evolved to give a highly realistic form of training for aircrews, so also are electronic warfare simulators now very realistic, very effective in training and very important. British Aerospace is a principal designer of this type of sophisticated system and offers a range of EW simulators of varying degrees of complexity to the navies of the world.

INTEGRATED ELECTRONIC WARFARE SYSTEMS IN OPERATIONS AT SEA

Since EW is now so significant in naval operations, we should consider how it fits into the overall perspective of a total ship's weapon and sensor system, and one concept of this has been put forward by MCD Pett (of the MEL Company). The summary of integrated EW systems in operation at sea which follows, owes much to that concept.

In the modern naval environment an increasing reliance is being placed on electromagnetic means for receiving and transmitting data, for command links, communication, surveillance and targeting purposes.

Effective interpretation and control of the electromagnetic spectrum enables rapid tactical decisions to be made by a centralized authority, in possession of information from numerous sources, in response to a dynamically changing threat environment. The monitoring of the spectrum by electronic support measures (ESM) and the denial of the intelligence-gathering process by electronic countermeasures (ECM) confers a strategic advantage during a state of crisis or conflict. Electronic-warfare systems are employed in order that a naval task force might gain such an advantage over a potential aggressor.

The threat can take many forms and can be recognized by its electromagnetic signature. The signature can be defined in several ways. Initially, a use of long-range patrol aircraft for convoy sighting is often a first indication of hostilities. Intercept of a scouting report from, for example, a hostile aircraft is an indication of localized and possibly intensified interest in a fleet, which may have been tracked by ocean surveillance means. Ocean surveillance may be carried out by shipbased, airborne or satellite means and the scouting reports will be probably sent at HF, VHF or UHF. The ability to monitor and localize hostile air co-ordination signals will greatly assist a task-force commander to assess the threat situation and develop his defensive or offensive tactics.

The second phase of intelligence gathering involves the detection and tracking of hostile transmitters in their surveillance or target-acquisition modes. At this stage of the combat, the transmissions will be in the RF spectrum from 1 to 18 GHz, or more. Their ranges may be as far as 500 kilometres for aircraft detection or up to 250 kilometres for surface vessels, perhaps extended by ducting phenomena.

The final phase is the identification of radars used for guidance of missiles. Such radars are often embodied in the missile as active or semiactive homing systems and may be turned on prior to launch from an aircraft or after launch when within a range of 20 kilometres of their target.

Other missiles perform their tracking using passive anti-radiation (RF) seeker heads or infra-red seeker heads. Such missiles can be detected either by using radar means (which aids the anti-radiation mode) or by passive infra-red surveillance methods to identify a locked-on threat by its own IR signature emanating from its engines and exhaust gases.

When a ship's radar is switched off, the role of electronic support measures is to identify passively the threat by recognition of its eletromagnetic signature. Thus the adversary is denied information about the ship's own radar signature, which could aid the enemy's surveillance and targeting functions.

Having identified the potential aggressor passively, electronic countermeasures can then be taken which may utilize active techniques to counter the intelligence-gathering activity in order to deny or delay the ability to act aggressively.

The primary objective of electronic warfare is thus to increase the survival of the ship and task force.

The requirements of naval ESM systems are common, whether dealing with a submarine threat, an air threat or a surface-vessel threat. The first requirement is the rapid interception and analysis of the RF emission. This analysis must be performed, even for the situation of a single sweep of a surveillance radar. Having analysed the emission, the ESM must classify the emission into either a friendly, hostile or unknown category and, if necessary, alert the command and control system.

The information provided must be reliable and make available, in the minimum case, bearing information to alert weapon systems if the ship's own active sensors have not established radar contact. The information must also be made available to the ECM system for response if so commanded. In certain situations where a lock-on threat is detected, the ESM may provide an automatic command to initiate jamming appropriate to the threat detected. Response times from detection, analysis and the initiation of a response in any direction will be less than a few seconds. By co-ordination with passive sensors on other vessels, triangulation is possible, both to permit coarse ranging and tracking of the threat.

In the initial phase of hostilities, the role of ECM is to deny or delay the gathering or transmission of intelligence by the adversary. This role is applied against communication links and surveillance or target-indication radars. The denial of information may take several forms.

In the simplest form, noise jamming on the frequency of interest can degrade the intelligence-gathering or transmission process. Against more sophisticated adversaries which are in a targeting phase, the presentation of alternative false targets can dilute the threat attack aimed at high-value vessels. The alternative targets may be created electronically by coherent false-target generation, by active off-board decoys, or by means of off-board decoys, such as chaff, infra-red decoys or active electronic decoys.

In the event of a missile locking on, electronic countermeasures must be able to achieve a break lock of the radar's tracking mechanism and seduce it from one's own ship. The break-lock capability must be effective, both in the situation where the missile is locked to one's own vessel, or in the situation where the missile is 'locked on' to a supported ship within the task force. A variety of sophisticated techniques are now available to accomplish this role, even against missiles having the most sophisticated target tracking mechanisms.

In its passive role, EW can provide detailed information regarding the signatures of intercepted emissions. This information can be used to supplement the information gathered from the ship's other sensors, e.g. radars, and thus differentiate friendly from hostile emitters. Because of the fast reaction time of EW systems, they can be used in conjunction with the control of the ship's weapon system to designate passively targets against which a missile launch should be effected.

Another major role of electronic warfare is the dilution of the threat in an attack situation. In the current scenarios of attack on a naval task force, it is possible that the attack may emanate simultaneously from several different bearings. This places an extremely onerous role on the ship's hard weapon system. However, by the use of electronic countermeasures, the threat attack can first be delayed by jamming techniques, thus enabling the point defence systems to concentrate on the high-priority threats. Secondly, after the missile launch has commenced, electronic countermeasures can cause the missiles' guidance function to be severely degraded, and so substantially improve the probability of survival in the event of a multiple-missile attack.

The system configuration adopted by the user will depend on a number of factors. The scenario will dictate the degree to which the EW capability will be implemented, as will the tactical role of the ship. It is possible that different vessels will be equipped with different fits to complement their hard weapon systems. Cost considerations will of course play an important role in the provisioning of an EW capability in ships.

In the simplest concept, an automatic radar lock-on warner, linked to a chaff system, may provide an effective means of defence against the terminal missile threat. In the most complex concept, where the role of the vessel is intelligence gathering, as well as the reaction by electronic means to the threat, a total solution to the electronic warfare requirements is needed. Several basic functions are:

The radar ESM system operating in the 1–18 GHz band with extension to 40 GHz and above

The radar ECM system complementary to the ESM function but primarily operating over 7–18 GHz, with extension possibilities both to lower and higher frequencies

The communications ESM system operating from 2 to 10000 MHz, with the possibility of extension to lower frequencies

The communications ECM system complementary to the ESM function operating over a minimum range of 20–400 MHz

The IR warner operating over the 3–5 micron band and optionally from 8–14 microns

Decoys and flares, which are used to complement the active ECM system and cover similar frequency ranges.

All sensors indicated require antenna systems for intelligence gathering and jamming transmission. For the reception of the intelligence, antenna arrays covering 360 degrees in azimuth and having elevation coverage to 40 degrees or more are essential to ensure a high probability of signal interception. The use of interferometric techniques over a limited sector of, say, 90 degrees is used to give high accuracy DF for passive-tracking.

The transmitter antennas must have high gain in order to maximise the effective radiated power used in the jamming process. The current concept is to use either a number of discrete fast slewing high-gain antennas, or to use a multibeam approach.

The next function is the receiving and transmitting function. Naval ESM receivers may take several forms, but, for the most sophisticated requirements, high-integrity wideband receivers are essential. To realise this, the IFM technique using binary processing is unparalleled in its data-processing capability in a hostile environment where threat parameters and tactics are changing. This may be supplemented by the use of advanced processing techniques to enable offensive jammers or CW transmitters to be categorised and eliminated from pulse-sorting routines.

Transmitters generally employ wideband high-peak, or medium continuous-wave, power travelling-wave tubes in the 1–18 GHz frequency band, or solid-state amplifiers below 1 GHz.

Dedicated processors are used to control the individual electronic-warfare system activities. Each has to undertake several dedicated functions, which include signal sorting and de-interleaving, signal measurement, signal analysis and the implementation of special techniques dependent on the system function. All data are made available via a data bus to a central computer for the EW picture compilation on one (or more) dedicated EW displays. Furthermore, these data can also be made available to other tactical-command functions.

In addition to the data-bus flow of information, there will be dedicated links between certain functions, e.g. a direct radar ESM to ECM link for lock-on warning designation, and a direct link from ESM and ECM to the decoy and flare launcher.

Digital and analogue recorders are an essential feature of the current EW suite to enable post-mission analysis to be performed on intelligence gathered during periods where the EW suite may be unmanned or where complex emissions require more detailed analysis than is available on board.

The ship's data bus will interface with the central EW computer to make available EW information to supplement that available from other sensors. Interfaces are shown to the control, command and communication station, to the anti-submarine warfare station, to the anti-aircraft–warfare station and to a data link to other ships' EW systems for triangulation purposes. The names used here are not necessarily those employed in all navies but serve to illustrate the EW interface function.

The use of electronic warfare has to be considered as part of the overall tactical defensive and offensive role of the ship's weapon system and be complementary to the role of the ship's other sensors and point defence systems. This permits the surveillance of the environment in radar silence to gather both tactical and strategic information of the disposition, identity and range of electromagnetic emitters, and thus gain a strategic superiority. In addition, it is possible to augment considerably the ship's fighting capability by diluting the threat and by delaying the onset of acts of aggression using active countermeasures. In the complex naval environment envisaged for the 1980s and 1990s, the use of integrated electronic-warfare systems is now seen to be essential to enhance the survivability of individual ships or the task force.

MODULAR DESIGN OF HARDWARE AND SOFTWARE

To provide flexibility in equipment design and to assist in creating a quick reaction capability to provide EW facilities to meet the different needs of various classes of ship and various threats, a modular approach is being taken by industrial designers. These modules enable a cost-effective tailoring of system design to be made to match the needs of any size of warship and any operational requirement for EW. Powerful automatic data processing and an ergonomically designed range of colour display consoles produce good man-machine interfaces to give the best operator effectiveness particularly in dense signal environments. These modules give an impressive array of system capabilities which can be assembled in whatsoever combinations are required, and they include, for example:

A capability to operate effective ESM in severe signal environments from surveillance radars, missile radars, own ship radars and other emitters.

A frequency coverage of at least 2–18 GHz with lower and higher frequency extensions associated with wide-open 360 degree aerials or scanning aerials and 100 per cent intercept probability.

A capability to provide passive targeting for weapons.

Radar libraries of many modes and automatic recognition of at least 144 specified threats as well as a radar tracking capability of many separate tracks and continuous automatic monitoring of the complete ESM system.

Colour displays for bearing/frequency presentation and for alpha-numeric presentations. Audible outputs to assist signal interception and give alarms. 'Operator friendly' keyboards and roller-ball controls to position cursors on the displays.

Very comprehensive radar analysis facilities both automatic and normal. Data logging and recording facilities.

Interface facilities for integration with the ship's command system and facilities for the automatic reaction to, or passing on of information on specified threats.

These system characteristics can be assembled in a building block fashion into EW systems for mine layers, MCM boats, fast patrol boats, missile boats, corvettes, frigates, cruisers, aircraft carriers and submarines.

For ocean going vessels, ESM is a prime sensor in today's maritime environment. Considerable strategic advantage can be obtained by maintaining EMCON policies by operating in a passive mode with own radars switched off. In this situation only the best ESM can provide the assurance of maximum operational effectiveness.

Here the EW operator needs the support not only of fully automatic, high integrity equipment but also the ability to monitor directly the 'real time' environment on the situation display and with audio.

The modular ESM offers this and in addition:

Fully automatic processing plus operator intervention
Advanced pulse train de-interleaving and identification
'Real-time' display of emitters plus synthetic symbology

Library extension, frequency extension and passive targeting modules are available either now or as a through-life upgrade.

Today the submarine plays a unique and important role in maritime operations. However the submarine must remain invisible to carry out its covert missions. At times when the submarine comes to periscope depth, either to snort or to communicate, it is essential that the masts should not be detected by ASW search radars.

Several ESM options fulfil all operational requirements of the modern submarine:

Warning of possible detection
Surveillance and identification
Passive targeting
Intelligence gathering

The ESM warning capability can be configured to predict any possible radar detectability of a submarine depending on the frequency of the radar, the sea state and the mast configuration. This is Reciprocal Intercept, as discussed earlier.

The threat to the submarine is from surface ships, maritime patrol aircraft and maritime patrol helicopters. Radars are used to optimize the detection of a submarine mast or wake in the sea. ESM is able to flag the presence of radars with complex modulations and provide a warning should the radar be capable of detecting the submarine. A 'snapshot' facility means the ESM antenna need only be raised for a few seconds. All data collected is stored and can be analysed at the ESM console with the mast lowered.

These capabilities of modern modular naval EW equipment show how far it has now developed in sophistication and complexity. Because of its operational value to modern navies, there is now a substantial world market for this type of equipment.

7

Electronic Warfare in Merchant Ships

Within recent years, some merchant ships have been attacked with missiles when acting in support of warships during the Falklands War or when in the Persian Gulf during the current war between Iraq and Iran. This has led to consideration of how such vessels might be given a measure of protection. Electronic warfare defence has featured extensively in these discussions because it is politically more acceptable than arming merchant shipping with guns or anti-missile missiles. Furthermore, it is considerably less expensive.

This represents a radically new approach to the application of EW and one that is well suited to non-aggressive defence. But it does pose two major problems. First, the very large radar echoing area of a big tanker makes it difficult to seduce a missile off the ship target, or to move the centroid of the ship-decoy echo away from the centre of the ship. Secondly, any necessary associated warning equipment to detect and identify an impending missile attack, especially at night, must be effective, automatic and reliable to be fitted in a ship whose crew have little or no electronic or tactical skill. It must, with a very low false alarm rate, indicate when to launch decoys, or initiate launching automatically. If the false alarm rate is too high the available stock of decoys would be wasted. This all means that very large decoys would be required to achieve any effectiveness, and quite a sophisticated warning and identifying equipment would be needed. The total cost, though less than that of active weapons, could be substantial nevertheless.

Of course, some reduction in missile lethality could perhaps be gained by taking relatively simple precautions concerning ship visibility and radar detectability, but the problem of protecting a VLCC to a significant degree by radar decoys is not simple. Ideally, what is required is an EW method which could be switched on continuously when the ship is in a danger zone and which would not run out of expendable 'ammunition'. This points to the need for some form of electronic rather than expendable decoy solution for radar-homing missiles. Unfortunately a masthead sea-reflection decoy of the type discussed earlier would not be suitable against sea skimming missiles since these do not steer themselves in the vertical plane, but use a radio altimeter to keep them at a fixed height above the sea, as we have seen earlier. Thus, a decoy which operated on pulling the missile off in the vertical plane would not be effective against this type of missile.

Applying electronic warfare measures to merchant ship protection is a significant new role for EW and is currently exercising the minds of industry as well as arousing the interest of marine insurance organizations, who might well reduce premiums for ships with some measure of protection. Ship operators are also interested for, apart from preserving their assets in the vessels, a measure of EW protection is also of benefit in sustaining the crew morale when the ship is operating in areas of potential danger.

Altogether this new requirement constitutes a different engineering system problem for EW designers accustomed to warship needs, and it also constitutes a new market for electronic warfare equipment. It is the first case, in modern times, where warship equipment has a role in merchant ships and it is, in a way, reminiscent of the arming of merchant ships with guns against submarines in World War II.

Consideration has been given to creating a self-contained merchant ship decoy system in a standard 40 foot ISO cargo container which could be carried on the deck of a ship like a normal cargo container. The 40 foot container could contain decoy launchers, missile warning receivers in an office for an operator, ready-to-use lockers for decoys and an engine-driven generating set to supply power. In this way it would be quite independent of the power services of the ship and installation would be very simple in merely loading two or four such containers on the upper deck of the ship. The operators, who would need to be trained, would decide when to fire decoys from the warning information of the sensors in the container.

The effectiveness of such an arrangement could be enhanced by the application of radar absorbent material (RAM) to parts of the ship's superstructure. By taking this measure, the radar echoing area of the ship, or the part of it treated with RAM, would be reduced and the required size of a decoy echo to be comparable would also be correspondingly reduced.

This would ease the problem of finding an effective decoy for merchant ships with large echoing areas, or it would make existing decoys more effective. However, the application of radar absorbent material to large areas of the hull or superstructure of a merchant ship is not a simple nor inexpensive matter. RAM needs to have a thickness of about 1 or 2 millimeters for typical missile homing radars. It is applied either in the form of sheets of linoleum-like material or as multiple layers of paint to build up the required thickness, which is quite critical. Sticking on the sheets or applying many coats of the paint is slow, laborious and expensive if the entire hull is treated.

It could be applied selectively to the upper parts of the superstructure which would be the first parts of the ship to be seen by the missile. This could bias the homing point of the missile to or towards a nearby decoy, before the full size of the total hull echo came into the missile's view and so possibly lead to an early selection of a decoy by the missile. But if the missile did not use radar homing until it was quite close to the target and could see more than the upper parts of the superstructure, a partial coating on the upper levels would probably be ineffective. Thus, the use of RAM on big ships cannot be seen to give guaranteed protection. Problems are also posed in the use of infra-red decoys particularly in the case of tankers where the presence of pyrotechnic devices on or near these classes of ship is generally not welcomed for obvious reasons, and all current infra-red decoys are based on some form of pyrotechnic.

There is no doubt that electronic warfare potentially could make some contribution to the safety of a merchant ship in such ways, but careful simulation and assessment would be necessary to see if the actual size and type of merchant ship concerned could derive worthwhile benefit from the use of the particular decoy proposed, supplemented by any other measures such as the use of RAM.

Smaller ships would certainly be easier to protect than larger ships but figures of effectiveness could only be obtained from an analysis of actual ships concerned and decoys proposed. Here a total self-contained package approach is needed and the merchant ship should be offered by industry a combination of equipment, skill and experience in trained men, and structural modifications such as RAM or camouflage paint. All these elements may be needed to make a worthwhile contribution, and furthermore the ship owner and insurer will need to be convinced that the cost involved would be well justified. So the EW industry needs to assemble a new set of capabilities which would include:

> A means of estimating the radar and infra-red target size of a ship from its drawings or model. This could involve model ranges, which do exist in industry in the UK.
>
> A simulation capability to explore the effectiveness of EW devices for particular ships, knowing their target size and the value of structural changes, possibly involving RAM or paint.
>
> A study capability to consider the geographic routes involved for the ship in question and investigate optimum tactics.
>
> A reserve of skilled staff to operate and maintain the equipment and supplement the experience available in the ship's complement.

It is clear that while EW may well have a role to play in merchant ships, it is not simple to determine nor necessarily easy to achieve. Cost-effectiveness is very relevant and requires expert assessment to see if it is worthwhile. The actual fitting and structural modifications to the ship are not negligible. While there are undoubted new opportunities for EW in merchant ships, a new approach is needed by industry, and a number of companies are indeed assembling the required capabilities.

Within the next decade, it should be seen whether there *is* a significant role for EW or not in these ships; to date, no positive reports are available of a successful defence achieved by EW in a commercial ship though unsubstantiated claims have been made. If a successful and viable package of EW measures is achieved, then, of course, it would be applicable to Fleet Auxiliaries and navies would in this way benefit through the transportation of their electronic warfare capabilities into the civil field.

One commercial system for the protection of merchant ships offered by the Marconi Defence Systems Company meets the requirement given above that a decoy should be electronic and of indefinite duration. It uses a noise jammer in a boat towed behind the ship to screen the primary target (the ship) and induce the missile to switch to 'home-on-jam' and steer itself to the decoy boat. This decoy needs no operator and is automatic in its operation. It is also much superior to using a towed boat fitted only with corner reflectors, as some merchant ships have been using. The Marconi Defence Systems decoy is designed to detect the radar and transmit a signal to break the missile's lock on the ship and force it to home onto the decoy instead. The interaction between decoy and missile is complex and the analytical and development work involves detailed expertise in both EW techniques and guided weapon homing. This active decoy is claimed to provide effective protection against EXOCET. It has been designed as a low cost solution to this specific threat.

As indicated above, the decoy is designed to be fitted into a small boat towed astern of the ship to be protected. The boat should be equipped with radar reflectors large enough to present a valid target to the missile. The decoy automatically detects and jams the missile, forcing it to home onto the jamming source. As the missile approaches the decoy

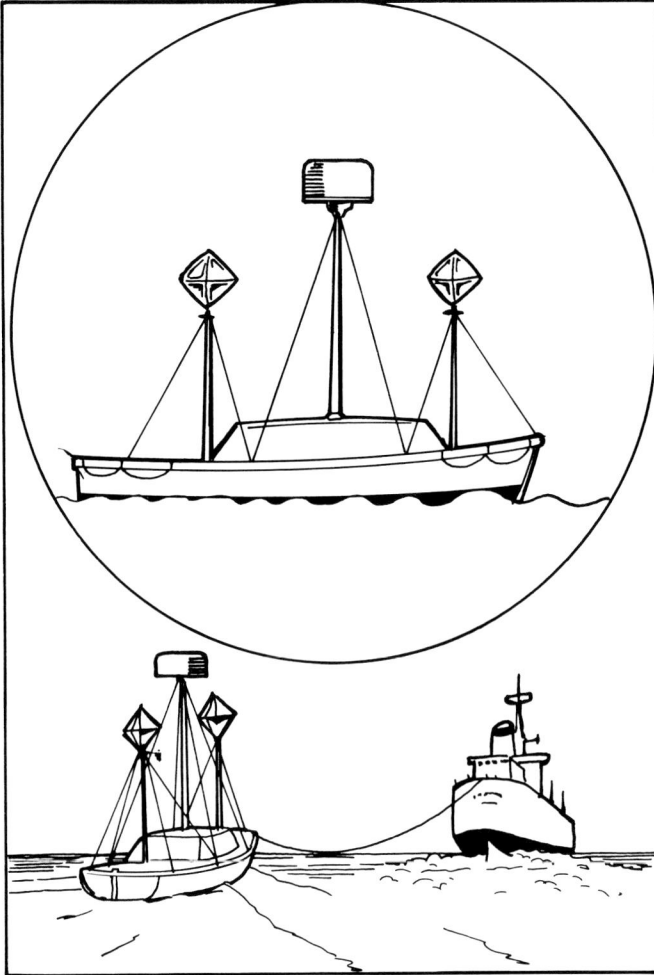

FIG. 7.1   Towed Decoy for Merchant Ship Protection *(Marconi Defence Systems)*

its radar will 'burn through' the jamming and see the radar reflectors on the boat and continue to home on to it. From the moment of decoy switch-on, the missile is unable to see its intended ship target. Instead it will be seduced onto a wholly valid alternative target.

A boat fitted solely with radar reflectors may prove adequate, providing the missile locks onto it and does not see the larger alternative echo afforded by the ship. While this is possible in certain circumstances, it does depend on the missile approaching from a specific threat sector and of course this cannot be assumed. It is therefore more effective to install an active decoy, as it will provide a far greater measure of protection.

The decoy which is installed in the small boat towed astern of the ship does not require an operator. The antenna is mounted inside a radome sited on top of the mast at a height of about 6 metres above sea level. The waveguide and multi-core cable run down the mast to the electronics unit located in an environmentally protected box in the bottom of the boat. A second box contains the power convertor which is connected to the rechargeable batteries.

The system has been kept as simple as possible to provide good reliability, reduce cost and minimise maintenance requirements. The user operates the decoy by switching it on and a tell tale lamp indicates that it is working. The decoy is powered by re-chargeable lead/acid batteries and needs no external power supplies.

Maintenance is carried out using normal field service test equipment and a full system check is achieved with a high PRF signal generator. Individual components can be repaired by replacement at first line with more complex work being done at the manufacturer's factory.

The approximate weights of the units are:

    Antenna Unit—5 kilogrammes
    Electronics Unit—10 kilogrammes
    Converter Unit—25 kilogrammes
    Battery Unit—180 kilogrammes

This decoy system is a genuine automatic device which needs no attention. It can be deployed and switched on for the duration of the ship's passage in dangerous waters.

8

The Way Ahead for Naval
Electronic Warfare

In addressing the question of the way ahead for electronic warfare it is perhaps more relevant to consider the future form of naval weapon systems as a whole. Major changes are taking shape and, while it is purely speculative, it is not unlikely that these changes will embrace and include electronic warfare. The trends are set and already apparent. What is happening is a process of integration whereby, to achieve a faster appreciation of the environment and a faster reaction to threats, the sensors and weapons are being brought together into a largely software-controlled single system. The separate concepts of individual sensors—radar, sonar and ESM— linked into a command system which then recommends to the Command the allocation of separate weapons to threats, is a form of naval system which is passing. It is tending to be replaced by a greater degree of automation in which the decisions on threat identity, the allocation of weapons to them and the firing of the weapons will be carried out largely by software.

The growing dependence of navies on software has been apparent for some time. Indeed, software is now vital to a wide range of applications, including command and control in ships and ashore, automatic weapon operation, engine room monitoring, logistics, data store and retrieval, intelligence processing and the management of displayed information of all kinds in ships and shore establishments. This application of software has occurred really over the last two decades and at an increasing pace in the later years. It is interesting to see why this has come about, and what the particular results are which have led to such a widespread use of and dependence upon, software in Naval circles. For tactical and operational applications, it is due to five main factors:

The speed of weapons and of war is increasing, the required reaction time is shrinking and there is little time for human decision-taking.

The volume of information from modern sensors is increasing rapidly and it cannot be appreciated or examined by human operators in the short times available or with the endurance of processors to long periods of operation.

Intelligence can be dispersed and delegated to weapons systems as processors and memories become more and more compact.

A wide range of design flexibility is provided by software. The functions performed by a given piece of hardware can be changed quite dramatically simply by the insertion of a new software programme.

The logistic support of the hardware in these systems can be greatly simplified. An equipment can be based on a limited range of common digital electronic modules, each one performing a different task under the control of its particular application software.

For non-operational applications, the advantages of software for navies are generally the same as those in civil fields—men can be replaced by automation and large quantities of information can be managed more rapidly to give increased efficiency.

In a peacetime volunteer-Navy, faced with financial restrictions, there are strong pressures to reduce manpower. This implies an increasing use of 'intelligent' machines. It is interesting that there is now a need to make advances in the ability of the user to specify, consistently, accurately and economically, what he needs in order to achieve the in-service benefits from this increasing investment in software. Application is thus not limited by technology but by the lack of a suitable type of language to say what is wanted.

In a modern frigate, there can be more than 200 significant processors doing different tasks in the weapon, marine equipment and ship housekeeping systems, which may give some impression of the extent of use of software in the Navy today. For example, a Type 23 frigate has 220 processors (thirty-five for marine equipment, forty-eight for its command system, forty for communications, fifty for its weapon system, forty-one in the weapons and six for administration). The first beginnings of automatic weapons in which the decision to fire is taken not by man, but by software are now at sea.

The first all-missile ship, the Type 22 (Broadsword) class frigate has major weapon system computers on board. The use of these computers in ship weapon systems varies from Action Information Organisation (AIO) systems, which co-ordinate, process and present real-time information supplied by the numerous ship sensors, to fully automatic weapon systems. The SEAWOLF System which saw action during the Falklands Campaign is supported by five computer suites with a combined storage of over 100 thousand words. The surveillance radar computer processes the radar target data on a pulse-to-pulse basis to provide the track data which is then used by the computer to formulate the threat to the ship in accordance with pre-set rules. Data from the most threatening target is automatically passed to the tracker computer, which controls the tracker during the search and acquisition phases, the servo loop being closed within the computer. Once locked on, the tracker computer automatically fires the missiles to anticipate a maximum-range engagement with a separate computer producing the corrective commands to the very agile missile to keep it on its intercept course.

Similarly, the VULCAN PHALANX Close-in Weapon System employs a computer to process the radar information, carry out Threat Evaluation and Weapon Allocation, automatically initiate the rapid firing gun into action and, using radar information, control the gun to ensure coincidence of the target and bullet stream. Again, a fast acting real-time computer of some 32 kilobytes storage capacity is used.

This trend can lead to electronic warfare losing none of its importance in naval capability but losing its separate identity, as is also likely to happen to the other elements of ship weapon systems. It is interesting that the great and rapid growth in naval importance of EW has been characterized by it becoming a separate subject in its own right. Now, its further evolution may lead to it being absorbed into a complete ship weapons system, largely software controlled, which is designed from the outset as a single entity using as ingredients the capabilities of the separate sensors and weapons of today.

This trend in system design is virtually inevitable as in future there will not be enough time in major operations for men to appreciate the tactical situation from sensor information and then decide to commit weapons to individual threats. What is likely to occur is the creation of a total ship system where the sensor information is appraised by software, and weapons, decoys and other ECM measures are deployed automatically. Already some EW systems have software control to the degree that decoys and other ECM devices can be launched and initiated from the ESM information automatically.

So, the future trend could well be that the complete weapon system for a ship would be designed as a single entity and would include and embrace a combination of radar, ESM, ECM and weapons, controlled largely by software.

Electronic warfare, as a separate discipline would disappear and the present separate hardware entities of ESM and radar would be combined into a single naval sensor capability.

Within this integrated capability, the contributions made by ESM and ECM techniques are likely to be along the following lines, and the role which men play in this man–machine mix would be radically different from the position today. The role of men would be less and would be different, and it will need very careful definition in the ship weapon systems of the future.

THE WAY AHEAD FOR ESM

Apart from a general improvement in the performance of ESM components, which will come from the normal trend of better technology, the major change which is likely to come about is in the system architecture of naval sensors towards what could be termed a unified or integrated sensor. This would be facilitated by precise navigation information for all ships from the new GPS navigational aid and contain all the current information gathering equipments—radar, ESM, data links, AEW—for the surface battle. But with increased data handling there would be one display only on which all contacts would be shown together with their identity or possible identity. ESM would play a major part in this integrated display of information as probably the only source of target identity information. But to enable the ESM information to be adequately correlated with radar and other information, more bearing accuracy would be necessary and an additional second stage of precise EW DF could well be needed. With this integrated sensor system, the command would see all the available sensor information together in a consolidated form. There would be no separate displays for ESM, radar and other sensors and indeed the sensor integration would probably, and should, include information from sonar sensors to provide a complete picture of all contacts around the ship. This is the likely direction in which ESM systems will move, and in many ways it parallels the likely trend to integrate all the navigation sensors into a unified system called an electronic chart. Data handling units, with modern large scale integrated circuits, are becoming smaller, faster and cheaper and this, together with better DF accuracy, will be the main expeditors in new integrated sensor systems.

The way ahead for submarine ESM is rather different since large suites of integrated electromagnetic sensors are not involved as in surface ships but even so integration of sonar and ESM information onto a single display could well be of value to the appreciation of the overall tactical situation in submarines. The views and opinions which are forming the future characteristics of submarine ESM capabilities and equipments are well represented by the way ahead as perceived by the Sperry Company. They offer the GUARDIAN STAR design of submarine ESM to the navies of the world, evolving from today's submarine requirements to those of the future.

Today's pressing need is for a truly responsive ESM system for operational submarine forces, one that can assess the entire threat envelope and provide the highest probability of warning with the lowest possible false alarm rate, whilst minimizing the risk of counter-detection. Today's emitter environment is becoming increasingly complex and, at the same time, the density of emitters continues to increase. An ESM system must be more than just a simple radar video detector to provide adequate protection.

Whilst it is difficult to predict the future, certain trends are evident. Emitters are continuing to proliferate and their complexity is becoming more exotic; multiple agiles may become the norm with unique emitter identification codes also becoming common. As the cost of weapons platforms increases, their numbers may decrease but they will necessarily have to assume a multi-mission role forcing an even greater level of weapons emitter sophistication.

Threat detection in a dense electromagnetic environment presents a problem because ESM systems must remain fairly wide open to provide a high probability of intercept. Thus they are subject to being virtually jammed by high duty cycle signals and impeded from processing the rest of the environment.

In practice, the best solution is thought to be to integrate a wideband IFM based receiver with a narrowband superhetrodyne receiver. The wideband channel tracks the normal environment and passes high duty cycle or highly exotic emitters to the narrowband channel. At the same time the emitter is inhibited from the wideband channel allowing the environment to be continually tracked.

Location or DF also drives the future ESM system design. As the precision or accuracy requirement increases, so does the antenna aperture or overall physical size. More radar cross section is exposed thus increasing the risk of counterdetection.

Sperry has developed a unique antenna concept which allows automatic and accurate DF on every emitter in the environment whilst exposing the lowest possible radar cross section profile. The system continuously surveys the entire environment to provide a complete ESM picture as an integral part of its primary warning function.

The antenna radome is periscope-mounted containing both omni and DF antenna arrays. Other antennae can easily be integrated into the assembly for communications and navigation functions. A typical assembly has maximum dimensions of 36 centimetres high × 15 centimetres diameter with a weight of only 5 kilogrammes.

Analysis can be either manual or automatic using good digital practices. Manual analysis of wideband receiver data in a dense pulse environment is virtually impossible. Even some automated processors have difficulty handling high duty cycle and exotic emissions.

The optimum solution is thought to be to combine the best features of both wideband and narrowband receiving systems under the control of a properly structured processing system. High quality digitized IFMs can track all types of frequency agile emitters including pulse-to-pulse hoppers. IFM receivers can report the presence of frequency, phase, or amplitude modulations and CW. Batch modulations of combined agile emitters can be unscrambled by correct use of a narrowband channel. Operator initiated analysis can also be conducted on complex pulse emissions and exotic antenna scan characteristics. The secret is combining these facilities in proper hardware and software architectures under processor control with computer aided operator intervention.

Classification of emitters in today's cluttered environment is difficult. Either exceptional cognitive skills, or a uniquely structured digitized *a priori* library is required.

In practice two libraries are considered necessary. An *a priori* library containing known characteristics and another emitter mode library. The operator can thus relate signals to those in the library and also enter unknown unique emitter modes or parameters for instantaneous and ambiguity-free classification upon redetection.

Warning must be accomplished with the lowest possible false alarm rate. At the same time warning failures must never occur. If a submarine is detected the operational objective is compromised. If a submarine is unable to achieve the operational objective either because of detection or false alarms, the initiative is lost.

Warning remains the primary function of the ESM system with virtually 100 per cent probability of intercept and a near 0 per cent false alarm rate as essential characteristics.

To date it has been considered that accurate DF is best achieved by a monopulse DF antenna array based system. In such a system monopulse DF antennae must compare the instantaneous amplitudes of two adjacent antennae simultaneously using two completely different signal paths. These paths must be balanced and calibrated very precisely. However, the components age and degrade at different rates so that variations between signal paths can severely degrade DF accuracy. Some monopulse systems have six paths. Such systems also are bulky with a large radar cross section.

The Sperry system uses only one signal path which is rapidly switched around the DF array. After initial antenna pattern measurement and verification the DF accuracy of the system suffers no degradation. Imbalance has been designed out.

Software based equalisation techniques are used to ensure a highly accurate DF. Antenna correction patterns are not specific to a particular array, thus allowing the array to be changed within a matter of minutes should it suffer damage.

The designer has to be able to upgrade today's system without major redesign as the threat develops and new technology becomes available. Miniaturisation of RF components and VHSIC technology are of little use to the designer if he has not allowed for them in his system's architecture.

Equally, a submarine ESM system that is effective but has a large antenna array, or needs more than one array to accomplish the task, will not be effective against the next generation of radars. A new generation of weapons emitters is introduced at approximately ten yearly intervals. In fact, present ESM systems are not thought to have kept pace with radar development. Future radars will have excellent clutter rejection capability and be able to detect smaller objects in much higher sea states at greater ranges on the sea surface.

ESM is at a crossroads in submarine sensor technology. Soon intercept and optronics masts will become the rule rather than the exception. An ESM system must therefore be both modular and flexible enough to encompass future requirements and keep pace with developments by the process of enhancement rather than expensive replacement.

THE WAY AHEAD FOR ECM

Undoubtedly the way ahead for ECM lies in the evolution of more sophisticated radar and infra-red decoys effective against modern missile homing methods, and probably coupled to the ESM warning system. In this way the launching of the decoys could be automatic against recognition by the ESM of an identified threat signal. This would achieve the fastest deployment which is indeed necessary, though there must be a very low probability of false alarms. No other ECM device is so important as decoys and it could be said that ECM had now, through experience, been refined to one very cost-effective class of equipment, which is a most satisfactory state of affairs.

Self Test Questions

INTRODUCTION

1. Explain what Electronic Warfare actually is to a non-expert person.
2. How does electronic warfare differ from other forms of naval warfare?
3. What are the essential parts of naval electronic warfare and why is it so important in naval operations?
4. Why has the use of electronic warfare in naval operations a measure of political attractiveness in certain circumstances?
5. Discuss the principal differences between electronic and sonic warfare techniques together with their areas of similarity.
6. How far could electronic warfare be conducted without prior intelligence on an enemy?
7. Is electronic warfare likely to increase further in importance in naval operations, and if so, why?
8. Can you think of any parallels to electronic warfare in civil fields other than merchant ships?
9. Why are the details of electronic warfare carried out by any country secret?
10. Discuss the relative contributions of men and machines in modern electronic warfare in naval operations.

THE EARLY DAYS OF NAVAL ELECTRONIC WARFARE

11. When and how did electronic warfare begin in naval operations?
12. How was electronic warfare in its early days regarded by the Naval Command at sea and ashore?
13. What was the earliest significant success gained by naval electronic warfare in your opinion?
14. Could electronic warfare have played a greater part in naval operations in its early days, and if so why did it not?
15. Discuss the relative successes of the Germans and the British in the early days of naval electronic warfare during World Wars I and II.
16. What are the main operational advantages and disadvantages of scanning and non-scanning electronic warfare intercept receivers?
17. Should the technological foundation for electronic warfare equipments lie in industrial or Government laboratories?
18. Is there too much secrecy associated with electronic warfare to-day?

19.   As a commander at sea, would you place more importance on reliability or performance in naval electronic warfare equipment?

20.   To what extent does an increasing electronic warfare capability contribute to more cost-effectiveness in naval weapons and sensors?

PASSIVE ELECTRONIC WARFARE

21.   What unique tactical advantages are given by electronic warfare alone?

22.   How important would it be to have greater bearing accuracy, and why?

23.   Why is the intercept range greater than the radar range?

24.   What are the propagation modes which give long range intercept?

25.   Why does Reciprocal Intercept not depend upon propagation conditions?

26.   Describe briefly the main features of amplitude-comparison direction finding.

27.   Discuss the problems and the main techniques in signal analysis.

28.   Why is it reasonable to accept a relatively high measure of complexity and cost in passive EW equipment?

29.   Why is passive EW so particularly important to submarines?

30.   In which ways do you think passive EW should evolve to give even greater tactical advantages at sea?

ACTIVE ELECTRONIC WARFARE

31.   What are the two main objectives of active electronic warfare?

32.   What are the essential operational contributions made by noise jamming?

33.   Why does noise jamming involve a risk of danger to the jamming ship?

34.   Why do electronic false targets not contribute directly to reducing lethality of a missile?

35.   Discuss some of the principal forms of decoy.

36.   Why is it sometimes disadvantageous to jam communications transmissions?

37.   What are the functions of Confusion, Distraction, and Seduction decoys?

38.   Discuss two types of break-lock devices, their advantages and limitations.

39.   Discuss area and point defence in naval electronic warfare.

40.   What do you see as the main advantages in having active EW as well as naval surface weapons?

ELECTRONIC COUNTER-COUNTERMEASURES

41.   What are the principal anti-intercept measures which may be adopted?

42.   How could jamming be avoided.

43.   What anti-radar measures may be used?

44.   What types of missile are less prone to decoys?

45.   On what basic principles is STEALTH based?

46.   How does RAM work and what are its advantages and limitations?

47.   Why is a satellite sensor system important to navies?

48.   Discuss the significance of the ARM and its effect on the defences of warships.

49.   What are the problems posed by EMCON to the Command, and the potential advantages it can bring.

50.   Is ECCM ever likely to make ESM and ECM ineffective?

OPERATIONAL ASPECTS OF ELECTRONIC WARFARE

51.   How important is training in EW and how would you have it carried out?
52.   Should EW be a prime subject in all naval colleges?
53.   Is EW simulation important to invest in, and if so, why?
54.   How would you determine how much in a ship weapon system's cost should be devoted to EW?
55.   Discuss the importance of the man-machine mix and the role of the Naval Application Officer in an effective naval electronic warfare contribution.
56.   What are the basic contributions made by ESM, ECM and ECCM in a ship's operational capability?
57.   How would you use EW to gain tactical benefits in your own types of naval operations, and why?
58.   Should EW equipment remain separate or be more closely integrated into the overall ship weapon system?
59.   What are the advantages to a navy of having EW equipment constructed in the form of functional modules?
60.   In priority, what are the basic EW capabilities you would seek to obtain for ships in your navy? Why have you ranked them in this order?

ELECTRONIC WARFARE IN MERCHANT SHIPS

61.   Why is EW a good method of protecting merchant ships?
62.   What are the principal difficulties involved in using EW in merchant ships?
63.   As a ship owner, in what respects would you see an investment in EW paying a dividend?
64.   What special characteristics are desirable in merchant ship EW?
65.   As a shipowner, what questions would you ask of an equipment supplier before buying his product?
66.   Discuss any use of EW in a merchant ship of which you are aware.
67.   In what other ways, apart from those discussed in the book, do you think EW could contribute to merchant ship operations?
68.   How should the equipment supply industry prepare itself to serve the merchant ship market for EW?
69.   Discuss the relative merits of protecting merchant ships by installing EW equipment in them, or using warships to support them.
70.   Do you see any other potential civil applications for electronic warfare?

THE WAY AHEAD FOR NAVAL ELECTRONIC WARFARE

71.   Should naval EW become integrated with other sensors and weapons into composite ship systems?
72.   What are the main reasons why software is becoming so important and widespread in ship weapon systems?
73.   What are the operational and logistic advantages of a largely software-controlled ship weapon system?
74.   What will be the prime role of the naval officer in a largely software-controlled weapon system?

75.   What are the likely new capabilities in future ESM for surface ships?

76.   What is the probable way in which ECM will evolve in the future?

77.   How is submarine ESM likely to evolve in the future?

78.   Is the success of EW likely to reduce the use of electro-magnetic sensors in ships and weapons and encourage the adoption of other systems?

79.   Has electronic warfare made a permanent change in the pattern of naval operations or simply contributed to the earlier patterns?

80.   Successful ECM should have the minimum dependence on precise intelligence information or enemy weapon characteristics. Discuss this particularly in relation to future trends.

About the Author

Dr Kiely is a Consultant Engineer following his last appointment in the UK Ministry of Defence as The Chief Naval Weapon System Engineer.

A graduate of Queen's University, Belfast and of the Sorbonne, and a Fellow of the Institutes of Physics and of Electrical Engineering his career has been in the field of marine electronics both for the Royal Navy and for civil marine applications. He has also been much concerned with the methods and organization of large scale defence procurement, and devised and introduced the Cardinal Points Procurement procedure.

Dr Kiely's interests include fly fishing, gardening and the conservation of rare species; he is a member of the World Pheasant Association and a supporter of similar bodies.

Index